W9-BWN-430

"To Everything There Is a Season"

New Narratives in American History

Series Editors
James West Davidson
Michael B. Stoff

Colonial

Richard Godbeer   *Escaping Salem:*
                     The Other Witch Hunt of 1692

Southern

James E. Crisp   *Sleuthing the Alamo:*
                     Davy Crockett's Last Stand and Other
                     Mysteries of the Texas Revolution

William L. Barney   *The Making of a Confederate:*
                     Walter Lenoir's Civil War

Civil War and Reconstruction

John Hope Franklin   *In Search of the Promised Land:*
and Loren Schweninger   *A Slave Family and the Old South*

William L. Barney   *The Making of a Confederate:*
                     Walter Lenoir's Civil War

James West Davidson *'They Say':*
                     Ida B. Wells and the Reconstruction of Race

Twentieth-Century Environmental

Mark H. Lytle   *The Gentle Subversive:*
                     Rachel Carson, Silent Spring, and the Rise
                     of the American Environmental Movement

African American

James West Davidson *'They Say':*
                     Ida B. Wells and the Reconstruction of Race

John Hope Franklin   *In Search of the Promised Land:*
and Loren Schweninger   *A Slave Family and the Old South*

"To Everything There Is a Season"

Pete Seeger and the Power of Song

Allan M. Winkler

OXFORD

UNIVERSITY PRESS

2009

OXFORD

UNIVERSITY PRESS

Oxford University Press, Inc., publishes works
that further Oxford University's objective of excellence
in research, scholarship, and education.

Oxford   New York
Auckland   Cape Town   Dar es Salaam   Hong Kong   Karachi
Kuala Lumpur   Madrid   Melbourne   Mexico City   Nairobi
New Delhi   Shanghai   Taipei   Toronto

With offices in
Argentina   Austria   Brazil   Chile   Czech Republic   France   Greece
Guatemala   Hungary   Italy   Japan   Poland   Portugal   Singapore
South Korea   Switzerland   Thailand   Turkey   Ukraine   Vietnam

Copyright © 2009 by Oxford University Press, Inc.

Published by Oxford University Press, Inc.
198 Madison Avenue, New York, New York 10016

www.oup.com

Library of Congress Cataloging-in-Publication Data
Winkler, Allan M., 1945–
To everything there is a season : Pete Seeger and the power
of song / Allan M. Winkler.
p. cm. — (New narratives in American history)
Includes bibliographical references and index.
ISBN 978-0-19-532481-5; 978-0-19-532482-2 (pbk.)
1. Seeger, Pete, 1919–   2. Folk singers—United States—Biography.   3. Popular
music—United States—History and criticism.   4. Protest movements—United States—
History—20th century.   5. Popular music—Social aspects—United States.   I. Title.
ML420.S445W56   2010
782.42162'130092–dc22
[B]
2008043379

3 5 7 9 8 6 4 2

Printed in the United States of America
on acid-free paper

For Toshi

CONTENTS

FOREWORD

∞

WHAT SOUNDS THE TIMES? IS IT THE BELLOWING OF politicians? The roar of the crowd? The ebb and flow of everyday conversation? John Dos Passos answered these questions by writing the *USA* trilogy. In three masterful novels, he sounded the times of the first thirty years of the twentieth century, evoking its angular, often frenetic tempo through words on the page. As for the rest of the tumultuous century, Pete Seeger sounded the times with his music and lyrics perhaps better than anyone. The labor movement of the 1930s, the peace movement on the eve of World War II, the civil rights and antiwar movements of the 1960s, and the green crusade for clean water all bear the mark of Seeger's melodies and echo the rhythms of a century of change.

Seeger's songs do more than sound the times, as Allan Winkler shows in his "*To Everything There Is a Season*": *Pete Seeger and the Power of Song*. They flex a kind of musical muscle that shaped the times. We shouldn't be surprised. Songs have always moved people to action. They provided courage to Christian martyrs consumed by the fires of persecution, boldness to the French revolutionaries who marched on the Bastille, and defiant comfort to Jews bound for Nazi crematoria. For Seeger, folk music sang truth to power, even when those songs came wreathed in smiles.

Singing truth to power could be a dangerous business. "Rulers," Plato is said to have observed, "should be careful about what songs are allowed to be sung." Seeger learned as much in the hard school of life. An American aristocrat and a Harvard graduate, he turned his back on blue bloods and embraced the working class. His love of the underdog gave heft to his dream of reviving American folk music. In his eyes, folk music was the sound of America, and in the 1930s he hoped its strains would spark a "singing labor movement." The failure of the effort was more than matched by Seeger's success in helping to create the folk music revival that swept across the second half of the twentieth century.

As Seeger's own songs became anthems of activism, he paid a price for his beliefs. The anti-Communist witch-hunt of the 1950s damaged his career and shook his confidence but never broke his faith in the power of song. Seeger kept singing about injustice, whether in the twin scourges of racial segregation and discrimination at home or in a contentious war in Vietnam or in the degradation of the environment the world over. It was his special genius to marry words and music that inflamed more than one generation.

How precisely music moves us remains a mystery. How Seeger moved his listeners is no mystery at all. He understood that listening was not enough. He invited audiences to sing along, so that each voice joined with others, building to an emotion-filled climax and binding people together. His "hootenannies" transformed passive listeners into full-throated actors, no longer an audience but now a part of the medium *and* the message. In the process, Seeger turned the performer's "I" into a chorus of "we" with an enormous potential. Put another way, the physical act of singing together creates an imagined sense of community and involvement, the musical analogue of "participatory democracy" that can drive action beyond the stage, the concert, and the music hall. For those reasons several selections from the Seeger songbook accompany the hardcover edition of this volume and help to make it as unique an addition to the Oxford New Narratives in American History as Seeger's music is to American culture and politics.

James West Davidson
Michael B. Stoff
Series Editors

FOREWORD

THE PETE SEEGER I HAVE KNOWN IS ALIVE IN THESE PAGES, head cocked back and banjo pulling us all into another song, another chorus. Allan Winkler has created a biography of this one absolutely irreplaceable driving force behind the folk song revival in America. We can, and do, praise the Lomaxes, John and Alan, Woody Guthrie, and others, but, as Dr. Winkler shows convincingly, without "America's Tuning Fork" the revival would never have attained its full growth and power.

Pete Seeger was always our hero. Some of us in the late 1950s, at the University of Oklahoma, were madly learning every folk song we could find. We never thought that thousands of our contemporaries across the country were doing likewise—people like The Kingston Trio, for example, or Peter, Paul and Mary; Johnny Cash, Bob Dylan, and Joan Baez. Pete's Folkways recordings were the ones we sought out. We'd play a track and one of us would write the first line of the lyric, the other the second, etc. Usually it took a few times before we got it and then we'd try out the chords. Since most had only three or four chords, this wasn't too hard. Then we'd listen several more times to how Pete sang the song and try for his approach. Looking back, it strikes me that Pete never tried to convince us that he was "Appalachian" or black, Irish, African, or Scottish. He sang them in his own voice with a directness that made the song the star and the singer merely the presenter. It's an approach many of us took a long time to find; we found it hard to resist the urge to seem to be the lumberjack or cowboy.

What drew us to Pete was his idealism, his rock-solid conviction that this country needed to live up to its stated principles. He saw that music was an immediate way of bringing people together and that folk songs spoke most directly to the greatest number of people. When he sang "Deep Blue Sea," we sang it, too. It was a mainstay of our singarounds, as was "Delia's Gone," "Sloop John B.," and dozens of others. We didn't know who Delia was, or Willy, or the Sloop John B. We just loved their songs.

One day I dropped by my friend Johnny Horton's apartment in Norman. He had a basic mono hi-fi setup with a huge speaker. Some early tech genius had taken a blister from a B-29 bomber and set a tweeter and woofer within it, covering the opening with fabric. I don't know how it would sound now, but then it seemed a mighty speaker, indeed.

Johnny said, "Listen to this," and put a new LP on the turntable. Out came Pete's banjo introduction to "Darlin' Corey." What followed was a transforming experience for me. It was my first hearing of *The Weavers at Carnegie Hall,* and by the final track I was set on the path I still follow. This was, and still is, one of the greatest folk music recordings ever. In it there were examples of many of the forms this music embodies: there were children's songs, lullabies, political songs, songs of love and nonsense, ballads, peace songs, and more. It was an object lesson in the breadth of the folk music spectrum and has informed the repertoires of more urban folk singers and rock and country singers than one can count. Many times I've been asked why I write so many different kinds of songs and I can simply say, "I learned that from Pete, Woody and the Weavers."

One can see his influence everywhere. Together with Zilphia Horton and Guy Carawan of the Highlander School in Tennessee, he adapted the old hymn "We Will Overcome," and created the anthem of the civil rights movement, "We Shall Overcome." Can anyone imagine that life-changing movement without that song? He sang for the unions when to do so risked a broken head or worse; he sang in the face of HUAC and the red-baiters and McCarthyites; he sang for civil rights, for peace, and for the planet. Somewhere in all that singing, he must have sung for you. He still sings for me.

Tom Paxton

Acknowledgments

I'VE HAD A WONDERFUL TIME WRITING THIS BOOK. IT HAS allowed me to combine a passion for history with a longtime love of folk music. As the manuscript took shape I benefited from the comments of friends and colleagues who read various drafts and helped sharpen both the argument and the prose. Dennis Sullivan, a Miami University economist with whom I perform regularly, made a number of important observations, as did Dan Cobb, a young historian in my own department who also plays music with me frequently. Tim Lynch, a colleague at a neighboring college and the author of a book on strike songs of the Great Depression, read both the proposal and several drafts and provided useful feedback. Dave Edmondson, a teacher and musician, pushed me to reflect on Seeger's role as a performer. And Richard Campbell, the director of Miami University's journalism program, gave me essential encouragement as he read an early draft. I likewise appreciate the careful reading of a number of reviewers who received the manuscript from Oxford University Press, including Tracy Campbell at the University of Kentucky, Nancy

Gabin at Purdue University, Jonathan Rees at Colorado State University–Pueblo, Ralph Young at Temple University, Carol Sue Humphrey at Oklahoma State University, Timothy P. Lynch at the College of Mount St. Joseph, and Pam Pennock at the University of Michigan–Dearborn. My sister, Karen Winkler Moulton, a superb professional editor, also gave this manuscript her careful attention, as she has with previous books, and as always insisted on a clearer focus and tighter writing.

Kitama Jackson, Pete Seeger's grandson, generously let me look through the huge digital archive of photographs he assembled for Jim Brown's film *Pete Seeger: The Power of Song* and then allowed me to make copies of the ones I wanted to use. Most of them came from the collection of Pete and Toshi Seeger, and I am grateful for their permission to use them in the book.

I appreciate the assistance of Katie Laux, my research assistant in the early stages of this project, who helped gather materials. And my thanks to longtime friends Mark and Gretchen Lytle for their hospitality each time I came to the Hudson River Valley.

This book would not have been possible without the careful attention of the series editors, Jim Davidson and Mike Stoff, both friends from graduate school. Jim was the one who helped nurture the idea in its earliest stages, first over dinner at his home and later in follow-up conversations. Mike then took the text and helped me understand how to shape it into what I hope is a compelling narrative. He pushed me in ways I have never been pushed before, and his efforts made a real difference.

Brian Wheel and Laura Lancaster, my editors at Oxford University Press, have been helpful from the start in dealing with the numerous details of picture and music permissions and manuscript preparation. Christine Dahlin steered the book through the production process smoothly.

My wife, Sara Penhale, has been a constant source of support. She gave me a copy of one of Pete's books early in our marriage, with an inscription I cherish. Over the years, as she has listened to me talk about projects or play my guitar, she has given me essential encouragement from beginning to end.

Finally, I am grateful to Pete and Toshi Seeger for welcoming me into their home, working with me at every stage of the project, and giving me insight into the dynamics of a musical career. Pete offered me materials, talked with me willingly every time I visited, read the manuscript, and even agreed to our playing music together in what for me was a real treat. Toshi, who long provided the cement for Pete's career and still handles all the mail, made me feel comfortable just sitting in the kitchen or eating meals with the family and helped review a final draft of the manuscript on one of my many trips to the Seeger home. This book is dedicated to her, with thanks for all she has done—for Pete, for me, and for everyone else.

"To Everything
There Is
a Season"

PROLOGUE

❧

STANDING BY THE STEPS OF WIDENER LIBRARY AT ONE EDGE OF Harvard Yard, Pete was at it again. Tall, lanky, and not quite nineteen, he should have been in class. But college bored him, despite the fact that his father was a professor. Sitting stiffly in a lecture hall or anywhere else wasn't his style. He could just as easily have been lounging in his dormitory with the other children of privilege who made up much of Harvard University's student body. The future president John Kennedy was there, and so was the poet Robert Lowell. But Pete never felt comfortable around them, even though his blood was as blue as theirs, bluer by far than the Irish Kennedy's. Instead his friends were his political allies in the Young Communist League, the radical, self-appointed champions of the underdog.[1]

So there Pete Seeger stood, in the middle of the Yard, passing out leaflets on a cold winter day on behalf of those fighting a losing battle to save democracy in the Spanish Civil War. Didn't his classmates realize that in 1938 the world was going up in flames, that aggressive fascists were crushing freedom not just in Spain but across the globe? In Europe, the Germans were goose-stepping their way through Austria and Czechoslovakia. In Asia, the Japanese were gobbling up chunks of China province by province. And in Harvard Yard Pete Seeger was standing, leaflets in hand, trumpeting yet another cause in defense of democracy and the downtrodden.

Politics wasn't Pete's only passion. He loved hiking and camping and being outdoors. He enjoyed painting. Above all, there was music. From the day he was born, May 3, 1919, music was in the air and in his bones. His father, Charles, was a pianist, his mother, Constance, a talented violinist. During their courtship, his parents gave classical chamber music concerts in the parlors of New York City's aristocracy. When Pete was born, they wanted him to play, too. "You must take lessons," his mother told him as he grew older.[2] His father had a different notion. "Don't try and teach Peter how to read music," he said. "Let him find his own way." And that's what young Pete did.[3] That's what he would always do. He was not so much a loner as an individualist; never planning, he seized opportunities as they presented themselves, often to change his life; rarely mindful of society's constraints, he was always attuned to the needs of other people; occasionally stubborn, he was always caring.

As a boy Pete picked up instruments—an accordion, an autoharp—deliberately left around the house, and without any formal training learned to play them, as well as the piano, on his own. He later recalled, "[By the time] I was five I could bang out a tune on a whistle, a penny whistle or an autoharp or a marimba."[4] Pete loved music, but *his* music, not his parents'. And his music, at least at the start, was jazz. Few could escape its syncopated spell, cast across the decade of the 1920s with the improvised rhythms and soulful sounds of Dixieland bands. Born in the gaming houses of St. Louis and New Orleans, spread by black musicians like Joe "King" Oliver and Louis Armstrong, the music of the underdog became the sound of the times, bestowing its name on the whole raucous era: the Jazz Age.

Music excited young Pete, gave an otherwise shy boy a sense of confidence and, when he finally performed, a connection to others he rarely felt elsewhere. From the moment he picked up the tiny ukulele his parents gave him when he was still young and began strumming its strings, he warmed to its rhythms. It was, perhaps, one of the few moments of warmth in his childhood, a "very cold" one, he later remembered.[5] The family chill—a result of marital tension—forced him into a shell, unable or unwilling to reach out to people. Except when he performed. With ukulele

Pete as a young boy (Collection of Pete and Toshi Seeger)

in hand and friends joining in, he played sea chanties like "What Shall We Do with the Drunken Sailor" and became a different person. His eyes sparkled and his face glowed as he relished the attention the music drew to him. When the music stopped, he crawled back into his shell.

Pete was a loner as a child. He loved the outdoors, particularly at his grandparents' home in Patterson, New York, and spent endless hours by himself, playing Indian in a loincloth. When he reached the age of eight his parents divorced. At boarding school since four, he had seen them only on vacations. Now he saw them separately on those vacations. Both still lived in New York but on opposite sides of Central Park. Pete spent half of his time with one, half with the other. From his father Pete derived his deepest emotional support. "My father was the one person I really related to," he said. "For good or bad, I had very few relationships with anybody else."[6] Instead, "[I became] good at playing by myself."[7]

Charles Seeger was something of a rebel even in academic circles. Though an expert in harmony who became chair of his department at Berkeley while still in his twenties, his work on music in its social and historical contexts struck a sour note among his colleagues, who insisted that music be studied in its pure and pristine form without reference to the world around it. The faculty and the university's administration found him even more unharmonious when he dipped into radical politics and began to speak in support of the Industrial Workers of the World, the left-wing union that wanted to jettison capitalism and overhaul labor relations in the United States. As radicalism fell even further out of favor during World War I, Charles Seeger left Berkeley in a huff, about to be fired.

Pete playing as an Indian in the outdoors (Collection of Pete and Toshi Seeger)

Charles brought his family back to the East Coast, where he spent a year building a wooden trailer that he could haul behind their Model T car. The idea was that the family would travel around bringing music to rural Americans. Many years later, Pete would himself withdraw to build his own home in the hills, to give him a base from which to take his music to the rest of the country. But this time, as Pete observed, "the trip was a disaster." He himself couldn't remember much—he was only a year and a half old—but he knew that his mother, more comfortable in refined settings, wasn't happy on the road. Travel was awful, he recalled: "We almost got drowned in a flood and my mother had

The Seeger family trailer on the trip to the South (Collection of Pete and Toshi Seeger)

to wash my diapers in an iron pot over an open fire. Once I fell in the fire. If I hadn't been snatched up a second later, I would have been killed."[8]

In his teens Pete developed his own preferences. As close as he was to his father and as much as he admired the elder Seeger's principled political stands, Pete just couldn't become interested in the new, experimental music of Aaron Copland, Arnold Schönberg, and others that so intrigued Charles. The new music simply didn't resonate with Pete; its tones and rhythms sounded all wrong. But Pete did take a liking to another variety of music his father was exploring: American folk songs. Not yet respected in musical circles, folk music was only beginning to gain popularity in the 1930s. More than most, political radicals like Charles saw it as a genuine mode of human expression.

Poster for a Seeger family concert (Collection of Pete and Toshi Seeger)

In 1932, Pete arrived at Avon Old Farms, an exclusive private high school in Connecticut, on scholarship. It was there that he found an instrument to bridge his interests in jazz and folk music. A teacher had a four-string, or tenor, banjo, often used in playing Dixieland jazz and other tunes. Pete asked if he could pluck it, and then and there decided that he had to have one. "There's a master here who would like to sell his banjo to me for ten dollars," he wrote his mother. "Please, may I have it?"[9]

His mother, more concerned about whether he had received a pair of patent leather shoes she sent him, at first ignored the boy's request. But Pete persisted, and his mother finally listened. He got his banjo. Off he went to the Avon Jazz Band, where he was soon playing the songs of George Gershwin and other jazz composers. His brother, John, taught him how to sing harmony. He practiced the technique everywhere, even in chapel, where it was strictly forbidden. Rules sometimes had to be broken.

As for folk music, Pete loved its rhythms, its harmonies, its messages. He wasn't the only one. In the 1930s, a number of folklorists began to comb small towns to record traditional songs in danger of being lost. These, they contended, were real American music that reflected the homegrown values and mores of the country. Charles Seeger was caught up in this movement, and other radicals, who had frowned on such music in the past, now began to see its importance in anchoring the country to an authentic national identity at a time of crisis and flux.

The trouble was that Pete couldn't play these songs on his four-string banjo, no matter how hard he tried. He finally realized that the songs on the recordings he heard were all played on five-string banjos. His father suggested heading south to hear some of this folk music—and to listen to some five-string banjo players—in person. In 1936, just before Pete entered Harvard, father and son drove through the Blue Ridge and Smoky Mountains to Asheville, North Carolina, to attend the Ninth Annual Folk Song and Dance Festival.

Pete was entranced: "I discovered there was some good music in my country which I never heard on the radio. I liked the strident vocal tone of the singers, the vigorous dancing. The words of the songs had all the meat of life in them."[10] Returning to his father's home in Washington, D.C., he found recordings of what he had heard at the festival at the Library of Congress and listened to them for hour after hour. He slowed the turntable with his finger on the record so he could hear every note and follow each rhythm.[11] Then he painstakingly picked the same notes on a borrowed five-string banjo. He had no teacher or instruction book; he was entirely on his own. At Harvard, where he was also a scholarship student, he continued to learn alone.

Though playing the banjo was important, Pete never thought about music as a career. He dreamed of becoming a journalist. Working at a summer camp after his freshman year at Harvard, he met several socialists who had signed up to fight fascists in the Spanish Civil War. For a moment, he considered joining them. Like those volunteers, he wanted to change the world, but he thought he could be more useful by writing about it. "[I was] keeping my distance," he said. "I liked the idea of not actually being involved myself, but observing the action." Still, observing was never quite enough for Pete. He had to *do* something: "If someone had offered me a job as a reporter, though, I'd have jumped at it."[12]

At the end of his sophomore year at Harvard, his frustration with school peaked: "[I was] disgusted by what I felt was the cynicism of my sociology professor...who told us students..., 'You can't change the world. There are certain inevitable things going to happen. The most you can do is analyze the world and hope you can analyze it correctly.'" Such indifference was infuriating at a time when Europe and Asia were going up in flames.[13]

Pete was also irritated by the academic jargon he heard in class. Seeking out his professor in his office, he asked why sociologists could not use simpler language. More comfortable himself with natural, straightforward forms of expression, he was incensed by the candid response he received: to impress people. "If this is the sort that's teaching here," he thought to himself, "I'm not going to bother studying anymore."[14] Poor grades led to the loss of his scholarship, and he left Harvard before taking his exams, bound for New York City. With war looming abroad and underdogs floundering everywhere, Pete planned to write about politics and leave music making to others.

"Talking Union"

⚯

After leaving Harvard, Pete had to decide what to do. More comfortable commenting on public affairs than trying to change them, he wanted to write but wasn't ready to plunge into a field in which he had little formal training. Instead, he took a train to Sarasota, Florida, where his mother was living, and indulged a longtime interest by taking art lessons for a month. There he learned how to work with watercolors, in particular how to do a graded-tone wash with his brushes. Then he spent the next three months pedaling across New York State and New England on a beat-up bicycle. He knew he had to support himself and decided to use his newly sharpened artistic skills to make ends meet. With canvas frames and an easel strapped beneath the seat of his bike, he crisscrossed the backcountry roads.

As he passed through fields of crops, he occasionally stopped in a cow pasture to paint a nearby farmhouse. Holding a just-completed watercolor, he would knock on a door in what soon became a regular pattern. He told whoever answered, perhaps a young boy, that he'd painted a picture of the house and asked, "Would you like to see it?"

"Hey, Ma," the youngster at the door often yelled. "Some guy painted a picture of our house."

"Would you like to have it?" Seeger asked.

"Gee, what do you want, how much do you want?"

"Well, I'm just camping out," Seeger replied. "I could use some food. If it's going to rain tonight, could I sleep in your barn?"

"You don't smoke, do you?"

"Nope, I don't."[1]

And that way he managed to keep himself going all through the summer.

He knew that painting outdoor farmscapes would never be a permanent form of employment, especially in winter. He also realized that he was not a very good painter. Once in New York City, after his summer of drawing houses, an art teacher he knew asked him, apparently innocently, about his other interests. "Well, I play the banjo," Seeger replied.

"I've never heard you play the banjo," the teacher said, "but I'd suggest you stick to that."[2]

So the question remained: What to do? Earlier in his life Seeger had dabbled with the idea of being a hermit. Troubled by a world filled with what he saw as deprivation and hypocrisy, he dreamed of detaching himself entirely from it. He watched his father's growing involvement with the Communist Party but was uncomfortable with toeing the party's rigid line. Better to be alone in the woods, he sometimes thought, than to live among those who cared too little or cared so much. A chance conversation with a group of his mother's violin students scuttled the notion. "That's your idea of morality? You're going to be nice and pure all by yourself and let the rest of the world go to hell?" one of them said. "That seems kind of irresponsible to us." "I decided they were right," he later recalled.[3] He put aside his aversion to rigid party lines and while at Harvard joined the Young Communist League. Still, even as he was handing out leaflets in Harvard Yard, a part of him remained more interested in observing the world and reporting about it than working to change things.

Unfortunately, he had little experience with the journalism that he thought might be the answer when he left Harvard. In elementary school he had put out his own newspaper, the *Spring Hill Telegraph,* and in secondary school had started the *Avon Weekly Newsletter.* While at Harvard he and a fellow student edited a monthly journal called *The Harvard Progressive.* But that was the extent of his experience as a journalist.

After his summer sojourn he headed for New York City, a place he had always dreamed of living, and began to look for work. A friend who worked at the *New York Times* got him an appointment, but it led nowhere. On his own he telephoned George Seldes, a noted newspaperman and freelance author, who told him abruptly, "Quit bothering me....I've got work to do," and hung up.[4] Seeger might have found employment, even in the field of journalism, in more prosperous times. But in 1939 the devastating economic depression still ravaged the country. Ten million Americans remained out of work, despite the best efforts of Franklin Roosevelt's New Deal. It was not a good time to be looking for a job.

The folklorist Alan Lomax saved Seeger. Lomax was the son of John Lomax, a one-time English teacher and later a banker from Texas, whose true interest lay in folk songs. He spent his life tracking down singers and recording them. Some of them made fun of him. A rancher once told him, "Why, everybody knows those damn-fool songs, and only a bigger damn fool would try to collect them." Instead of a recording session, the rancher suggested, "I vote we adjourn to the bar."[5] Alan Lomax followed in his father's footsteps. Just a few years older than Seeger, he worked first with his father and later on his own to record traditional songs and stories in danger of being lost. He traveled tirelessly around the country, and later to other parts of the world, capturing the creative work and cultural traditions of hundreds of artists in order to make the recordings, stories, and films available to the world. He was the first to record Huddie Ledbetter, the great Louisiana musician and master of the twelve-string guitar, who became known simply as "Lead Belly." Among other things, Lead Belly wrote such classics as "Goodnight, Irene," "The Rock Island Line," and "The Midnight Special," and even sang his way out of prison, where he was jailed for murder.

Alan Lomax also recorded the legendary Woody Guthrie, an itinerant Oklahoma guitar player. In the 1930s, Guthrie's songs chronicled the suffering of the Dust Bowl refugees whom author John Steinbeck immortalized in his novel *The Grapes of Wrath*. And in the 1930s, it was Alan Lomax and his father who helped the Archive of American Folk Song at the Library of Congress, founded a decade earlier, grow into a major repository of American folk culture.

Years earlier, Seeger had met Alan Lomax through his own father when Charles Seeger was running music programs for the New Deal's Resettlement Administration in Washington, D.C. Pete spent the summer of 1936 with his father, just after graduating from high school. There he got to know the younger

Lomax, who had already made a reputation for himself as a song collector. The two shared a passion for the American folk past.

In 1939, facing hard times of his own in New York, Pete met up with Alan Lomax again. Lomax introduced him to people like Aunt Molly Jackson, a folksinger married to an Appalachian coal miner. The two lived on the Lower East Side of Manhattan. Seeger had listened to recordings of many of her union songs during his summer in Washington. Now he heard her sing protest songs in person. He was captivated.

Through Lomax, Seeger met Lead Belly. One day Lomax called Seeger and told him to grab his banjo. Off they went to another apartment on the Lower East Side, this one inhabited by the fabled folksinger. Strong and squat, Lead Belly was having a hard time making ends meet. At the time, the Lomaxes had recorded only a few of Lead Belly's songs. Although many of them later became classics, he was little known outside of the Mississippi Delta. His playing dates were usually reserved for colleges and schools, which paid little, or benefits for radical causes, which paid nothing at all.

Wearing overalls in an awkward effort to identify with the working class, Seeger at first had a hard time relating to the well-dressed Lead Belly. "There I was," he said, "trying my best to shed my Harvard upbringing, scorning to waste money on clothes other than blue jeans. But Lead Belly had on a clean shirt and starched collar, well-pressed suit, and shined shoes."[6]

Seeger nonetheless found himself fascinated by the man who "moved with the soft grace of an athlete. He had a powerful ringing voice, and his muscular hands moved like a dancer over the strings of his huge twelve-stringed guitar."[7] As he watched him

Lead Belly performing before a small group with his twelve-string guitar
(Getty Images)

play, and played along with him, Seeger saw that Lead Belly "was not the cleverest guitar player; he didn't try and play the fanciest chords, the trickiest progressions, or the fastest number of notes.... The notes he played were powerful and meaningful. But perhaps his genius was not so much in the notes he played as in the notes he didn't play. Often he accompanied a song with single big notes and practically no full chords.... Or he would use single bass notes and occasional single top strings."[8] Seeger, who was playing his banjo more and more, sometimes for pennies on Park Avenue, was still learning his craft and soon, like Lead Belly, picked up the twelve-string guitar and learned to play it the same way.

Music did not dull his political senses, and Seeger gradually found himself becoming more aware of the world around him and the efforts to make it a better place. He became involved once more with the Young Communist League he had joined during college. During the fall of 1938, he recalled, "I connected up with the YCL again." With time on his hands he got to know members of a radical artists' group involved with the league. Each week between twenty-five and fifty people met in a loft in New York City. "I don't remember very much political discussion," he said, "except we read the *Daily Worker*." That spring, tired of reading the Communist Party newspaper, he and others made a set of puppets to put on traveling performances in small communities in upstate New York during the summer.[9]

In August the troupe members found a focus for their efforts. Twenty thousand dairy farmers went on strike against two large milk companies that were keeping the price of raw milk unreasonably low. The troupe went from one strike meeting to another, dramatizing the farmers' plight. In one episode, Seeger "played the part of a cow who tells the farmer he's foolish not to get together with other farmers to demand a decent return for their labor."[10]

During intermissions he reluctantly sang songs, such as "The Farmer Is the Man That Feeds Them All." For the first time he began to write new words to old songs. Taking a cotton farmers' song from the 1920s with the line "Seven cent cotton and forty cent meat / How in the world can a poor man eat," he changed it to "One dollar milk and forty cent meat." He did the same thing with a number of other songs. "Writing songs," he said, "was a heady experience. The folk process was working for me."[11]

At that point, Alan Lomax intervened again. Seeger still had not found a newspaper job, and the puppet shows were no more profitable than painting farmhouses. A job as a porter at the 1939

World's Fair was little better. Seeger's banjo playing was improving, and Lomax recognized that he had talent. The musicologist told his friend, "Pete, what do you want to be an artist for! You ought to learn more about folk music."[12] In the fall, Lomax invited Seeger to work with him at the Archive of American Folk Song. In his new job Seeger catalogued archival materials, transcribed songs, and learned a great deal about folk music. Hardly wealthy on the $15 a week he earned, he lived modestly: "[I stayed] in an old rooming house around the corner and kept to myself. Saved my money and bicycled out to see my parents occasionally."[13] He also practiced his banjo in every spare moment.

Thanks to Lomax, an opportunity to perform publicly came on March 3, 1940. A number of the nation's best folksingers—Burl Ives, Josh White, Lead Belly, and the Golden Gate Quartet, among others—were singing at a midnight concert in New York to raise money for migrant farmworkers. Seeger waited in the wings of the Forrest Theatre, near Broadway, until it was his turn to appear. He sang "Ballad of John Hardy" and later recalled, "I played and sang it terribly. I didn't know how to play the banjo, I was playing it the wrong way, and my fingers froze up on me. Tried to do it too fast. Forgot words. Got polite little applause for trying, and retired in confusion."[14]

The evening turned out to be memorable for another reason. At the concert Seeger met Woody Guthrie. Seven years older than Seeger, Guthrie came from an entirely different background. From Okemah, Oklahoma, he had drifted to California with many of the other "Okies" uprooted by the dust storms of the 1930s. He sang in saloons, on radio shows, at union meetings and political rallies, all the while writing thousands of songs. In an era of rising working-class consciousness, Guthrie was determined to maintain a homespun appearance. Radicals across the country embraced him as a real proletarian, able to understand the troubles of working men and women. Seeger had learned about Guthrie several years earlier, when a friend mailed him a mimeographed songbook Guthrie had written called *On a Slow Train through California*. Impressed and intrigued, Seeger hoped to meet the working-class troubadour some day.

Guthrie's performance at the Forrest Theatre electrified the audience. "The hit of the evening," Seeger said, "was this little curly headed guy with the cowboy hat shoved on the back of his head and a pair of cowboy boots and he'd tell humorous stories and then sing a song" that he had written himself.[15] "His manner was laconic, offhand, as though he didn't much care if the audience was listening or not."[16] On occasion, Guthrie even cleaned his nails with his guitar pick. Listeners loved his simple earthiness—and the songs. Guthrie made it easy for people to follow him with songs that were authentic, lively, and tuneful, telling of the problems real people faced during the Depression. As Seeger observed, "One song after another was a revelation to this audience of New York City intellectuals."[17]

After Guthrie's performance a crowd formed around him. Seeger made no effort to push through, but later, at a party where patrons could speak to performers, Lomax brought his friend over and said, "Here. Woody Guthrie, I want you to meet Pete Seeger."[18]

Like so many others, Seeger was fascinated by Guthrie. As he put it, "I just naturally wanted to learn more about him." The two became fast friends.[19] Coming down to Washington from

Pete performing with Woody Guthrie (Collection of Pete and Toshi Seeger)

time to time for a booking, Guthrie got together with Seeger, and Lomax persuaded the two of them to compile a book of songs about people who were down and out. While Seeger transcribed melodies from Lomax's recordings, Guthrie worked at a typewriter tapping out notes about the songs. They finished the project only to find that publishers found it too radical. *Hard Hitting Songs for Hard-Hit People* did not appear in print for another twenty-six years.

Guthrie grew restless and took to the road again. He told Seeger he was off to visit his family in Oklahoma and Texas and invited his new friend to come along. "It's a big country out there, Pete," he said, "you ought to see it, and if you haven't got money for a ticket, use the rule of thumb."[20] With nothing to keep him at home, Seeger agreed to go, and the two set out in Guthrie's car.

The ascetic Seeger puzzled Guthrie. "That guy Seeger," he once admitted, "I can't make him out. He doesn't look at girls, he doesn't drink, he doesn't smoke, fellow's weird."[21] Guthrie, in contrast, drank (in barrooms and recording studios), married (three times), and chased every skirt in sight (wreaking havoc with his marriages and his family). On the road, the two musicians made a strange pair. "I was an intellectual from New England, and he was a self-made intellectual from a small town in Oklahoma," Seeger said. "He was determined not to let himself be changed....I was eager *to* change."[22]

A drawing of Pete (Collection of Pete and Toshi Seeger)

As they headed first south and then west, Seeger learned from Guthrie. Lead Belly had taught him about the twelve-string guitar. Now Guthrie gave him a sense of clean, simple rhythm. Guthrie sometimes played verse after verse without changing chords, but he made the simplicity work for him by keeping the beat going. It was a valuable lesson that soon marked Seeger's music as well.

Guthrie also taught Seeger how to support himself by singing in bars. When the two arrived at Guthrie's home, Guthrie decided to stay. Seeger realized it was time to move on, and Guthrie told him how to do it. "Pete," he said, "if you go into a bar, sling your banjo on your back but don't play it right away. Buy a nickel beer … and sip it as slow as you can. Sooner or later, somebody's going to say, 'Kid, can you play that thing?' Now don't be too eager. Say, 'Maybe a little,' and keep on sipping your beer. Sooner or later, somebody would say, 'Kid, I got a quarter for you if you pick us a tune.' Now you swing it around, play your best tune."[23]

Encouraged by Guthrie, Seeger set out on his own, riding the rails for the first time in his life. It wasn't easy. "The first train I ever hitched a ride on was in St. Joe, Missouri," Seeger said. "Up until that time I'd only thumbed along highways. Some professional hoboes assured me, however, that the only sensible way to travel was by freight. After lurking around the yards all night, I finally jumped on what I thought was the right train. After an hour of switching back and forth, I found I had been shunted onto a siding."[24] Worse was waiting. Jumping off another train, he smashed his banjo, his sole source of support.

In addition to the traveling tips, Guthrie provided Seeger with something much more important: a model for writing songs.

Guthrie was prolific. As Seeger observed, "He wrote verses every day of his life. Kept a notebook in his pocket and scribbled down an idea, wherever he was." He could turn out songs even on the road. "Woody," Seeger said, "you should know how much people like me envy you, your ability to write verses like this."[25] Guthrie borrowed lines or melodies from other songs, figuring folk music had always been flexible that way. Seeger learned from that example and became a borrower, too.

The connection with Guthrie had a lasting impact. "I learned so many different things from Woody that I can hardly count them," Seeger said. "His ability to identify with the ordinary man and woman, speak their own language without using the fancy words, and never be afraid—no matter where you were: just diving into some situation, trying it out....I learned from him how just plain orneriness has a kind of wonderful honesty to it that is unbeatable....On most days of the week, he was always ready with a joke. But if he felt mad about something, he would come out and say it."[26]

While still on the road, in Oklahoma City Guthrie and Seeger wrote a song together, "66 Highway Blues." It was Seeger's first complete tune and helped him embrace the collaborative process in playing with ideas for songs. Guthrie described how they worked together in an introduction to the song in *Hard Hitting Songs for Hard-Hit People*: "I had part of this tune in my head, but couldn't get no front end for it. Pete fixed that up. He furnished the engine, and me the cars, and then we loaded in the words and whistled out of the yards from New York City to Oklahoma City, and when we got there we took down our banjo and git-fiddle and chugged her off just like you see it here."[27] The song was simple:

> There is a Highway from coast to coast,
> New York to Los Angeles,
> I'm goin' down that road with troubles on my mind,
> I got them 66 Highway Blues.[28]

"Union Maid," a more melodic song with a more pointed message, came out of the same trip. It began with a lively, upbeat verse:

> There once was a Union Maid,
> She never was afraid
> Of goons and ginks and Company finks
> Or deputy sheriffs that made the raid.

Each verse ended with the same powerful refrain:

> Oh, you can't scare me, I'm sticking to the Union,
> I'm sticking to the Union, I'm sticking to the Union,
> Oh, you can't scare me, I'm sticking to the Union,
> I'm sticking to the Union 'til the day I die.[29]

Though Seeger copyrighted the song in Guthrie's name, Guthrie contended that they had written it together: "Pete and me was fagged out when we got to Oklahoma City, but not too fagged out to plow up a Union Song. Pete flopped out acrost a bed, and I set over at a writing machine, and he could think of one line and me another'n until we woke up an hour or two later with a great big 15 pound, blue-eyed Union Song."[30]

In September 1939, with Europe bursting into flames, Seeger was ready to head back east. He had seen something of America, was enthused by the folk songs he had learned and written, and was ready to make his way as a musician. He appeared at a few local gatherings and sang with Guthrie at an American Peace

Mobilization march in Washington, D.C., to protest the nation's drift toward war. Now music and politics went hand in hand for him. His time on the road had shown him tough conditions firsthand, and his experience singing with Guthrie had helped him grasp how songs could articulate working-class grievances and empower people to act on their own behalf. That realization helped propel him into the union movement, with songs serving as weapons to mobilize workers to bring about social and political change. From his father, Seeger had come to understand the difficulties of the working class in a corporate America more concerned with profit than anything else. The Great Depression, and his own difficulty finding work, sharpened his sense of how hard it could be to make a decent living. His travels with Woody Guthrie and the occasional benefit concerts in which he participated made him all the more eager to use music to try to mobilize workers to created a more egalitarian world.

The American labor movement came of age in the 1930s. After years of bitter struggle, President Franklin D. Roosevelt's New Deal recognized labor's right to organize, guaranteeing industrial workers the chance to bargain collectively with representatives they themselves chose. When the U.S. Supreme Court declared one measure unconstitutional, a new law reaffirmed the right of labor to bargain with management and specified the legal mechanisms for workers to select their bargaining agents. Even then managers resisted, leading workers to occupy factories in a series of sit-down strikes in the automobile industry.

For the Communist Party and other radical groups, the gains of the 1930s were not enough. They wanted nothing less than a more equitable reorganization of American society. Seeger found himself

Pete and Lee Hays performing together (Collection of Pete and Toshi Seeger)

sympathetic to that effort. He dreamed of a singing labor movement, in which music could foster a sense of community and class solidarity, provide workers with a kind of psychological space as they pondered dismal factory conditions, and sustain them when they went on strike and walked for endless hours on picket lines.[31] He wanted to encourage them to sing songs, new and old, that would make them feel part of an America that valued their contributions.

In New York, Seeger met a singer of similar political persuasion. Lee Hays was a big, burly man, a few years older than Seeger, who had recently taught at the Commonwealth Labor College in Arkansas, a communal organization that trained radical political activists, much like the Highlander Folk School in Tennessee. Fond of eating and drinking more than was good for him, he had discovered he could take old gospel hymns and transform them into union songs with a few simple substitutions. When the college closed, he came to New York to see if the songs might be useful to union organizers there.[32]

When he met Seeger, Hays suggested, "How about teaming up? I know some songs, and you know that banjo."[33] Seeger agreed, recognizing that his tenor voice provided a nice complement to Hays's bass. In December 1940, the two made their first public appearance at the Jade Mountain Restaurant in New York City.

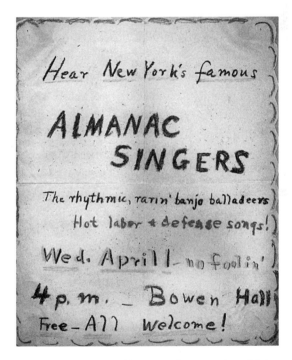

An Almanac Singers poster (Collection of Pete and Toshi Seeger)

Before long, Hays's roommate, Millard Lampell, a onetime college football player and now a radical writer, joined them. Others became part of the trio from time to time, including Woody Guthrie, comfortable with what he described as "the only group that rehearses on the stage." They called themselves the Almanac Singers, for as Hays said, "In the country, a farmhouse would have two books in the house, a Bible and an Almanac. One helped us to the next world, the other helped us make it through this one."[34] They performed at such gatherings as the radical American Youth Congress in Washington, D.C., and at left-wing functions around New York City.

The group moved into a large loft near Union Square. There they lived and worked together, sharing whatever money they made from performances or songs. They built a fourteen-foot picnic table around which friends gathered to talk or sing or have a meal. Sunday afternoon rent parties helped keep them afloat at a charge of 35 cents a head.

Though they shared the political sympathies of the Communist Party, most members of the Almanac Singers ignored the rigid hierarchical structure of the Party organization, and, as Seeger noted, "weren't actually members of any group."[35] Party functionaries frowned on what they felt was the casual style of the musicians. Nonetheless the *Daily Worker* gave the Almanac Singers a good deal of favorable publicity, headlining one story "America Is in Their Songs."[36] The author Theodore Dreiser declared, "If there were six more teams like you, we could save America."[37]

Lampell, Hays, and Seeger used the Guthrie technique of taking existing songs and shaping them to their own ends. Above all they wrote music that underscored their political beliefs. As much as Seeger and the others hated Adolf Hitler and the fascists in Europe, they clung to the Communist Party line that what was soon being called "the Second World War" was an imperialistic, capitalistic struggle that ignored the interests of the working class. Reflecting their aggressive opposition to American intervention, one song attacked FDR for pushing through the nation's first peacetime military draft. Sung to the tune of "Jesse James" and called "Ballad of October 16th," the chorus went:

> Oh, Franklin Roosevelt told the people how he felt,
> We damn near believed what he said,
> He said: I hate war and so does Eleanor but
> We won't be safe till everybody's dead.[38]

After that first musical effort the Almanac Singers wrote other antiwar songs and looked for a company to record them. As more and more Americans recognized that involvement in the war against Germany, Italy, and Japan was likely, the group found the popularity of its anti-interventionist message waning. Alan Lomax finally found a company, Keynote Records, that agreed to record the antiwar *Songs for John Doe,* but because of the inflammatory nature of the verses the record company distanced itself from the album, releasing it under the innocuous label "Almanac Records."

Distributed in left-wing bookstores around the country, the record received only modest and not altogether welcome attention. *Time* magazine, which still clung to its longtime isolationist stance, noted caustically, "Honest U.S. isolationists last week got some help from recorded music that they would rather have not received." What bothered the magazine was that the record alleg-edly echoed "the mendacious Moscow tune."[39] Carl J. Friedrich, a Harvard professor writing in the *Atlantic Monthly,* called the Almanac Singers "Poison in Our System" and said the songs were "strictly subversive and illegal."[40] First Lady Eleanor Roosevelt was reported to have found the recordings clever, "but in poor taste," and FDR himself, Seeger later recalled, evidently asked, "Can't we forbid this?"[41]

On June 22, 1941, in the midst of a rent party, the Almanac Singers learned that Germany had invaded the Soviet Union that day. Since the 1939 Nazi-Soviet nonaggression pact, the Communist Party had pressed for peace, but now, with Russia under attack, the party line shifted. Guthrie understood the implications. "Well, I guess we won't be singing any more peace songs," he said.

"You mean we have to help Churchill?" Seeger, now a mem-ber of the Party, asked about the British prime minister who was actively engaged in a war against Hitler that wasn't going well.

"Yup, Churchill says all aid to the gallant Soviet allies."

"Is this the same Churchill who said in 1920 we must strangle the Bolshevik infant in its cradle?"

"Yup, Churchill's flip-flopped and we've got to flip-flop."[42]

The Almanac Singers flipped without skipping a beat. No more anti-Roosevelt, antiwar songs; instead they sang about the importance of aiding the Allies and opposing the Nazis.

All the while, they continued to write the kinds of pro-union songs that first brought them together. One afternoon in the spring of 1941, Lampell and Hays were thinking of new verses for the tradi-tional talking blues Guthrie popularized in his well-known "Talking Dust Bowl Blues." Within an hour they wrote two-thirds of what came to be called "Talking Union." But then they hit a stumbling block: how to finish the song? At that point Seeger took over. Sitting on the roof of their loft with banjo in hand, he came up with an upbeat ending that contained a moral people could remember.

The song began:

> If you want higher wages, let me tell you what to do;
> You got to talk to the workers in the shop with you;
> You got to build you a union, got to make it strong,
> But if you all stick together, now, 'twont be long.
> > You get shorter hours,
> > Better working conditions.
> > Vacations with pay,
> > Take the kids to the seashore.

In verse after verse, "Talking Union" described how to start a union: pass out leaflets, call meetings, resist the attempts of the boss to derail those efforts, for "he's a bastard—unfair—slave driver—Bet he beats his own wife." Finally came Seeger's punch line:

> If you don't let Red-baiting break you up,
> If you don't let stool pigeons break you up,
> If you don't let vigilantes break you up,
> And if you don't let race hatred break you up—
> > You'll win. What I mean,
> > Take it easy—but take it.[43]

"Talking Union" was a near-instant hit. In 1941, the Almanac Singers recorded the song on an album of the same name and sang it wherever they went. It was one reason the Congress of Industrial Organizations (CIO), one of the nation's first organizations of industrial workers, agreed to sponsor the group on a national tour of CIO unions.

Just as the Almanac Singers were about to leave New York City, Guthrie returned from a stint in the Pacific Northwest. "Woody, how would you like to go west?" Seeger and the others asked. "I just came from the West," he replied, "but I don't guess I mind if I join up with you."[44] In need of money, they quickly recorded two albums of folk songs and with some of the proceeds bought a used Buick and headed toward the Pacific Coast.

On their summer tour, they sang at a maritime convention in Ohio and in such cities as Chicago, Milwaukee, and Denver. When they arrived in San Francisco, they faced a thousand longshoremen. "What the hell is a bunch of hillbilly singers coming in here for? We got work to do," they said. But after hearing "Union Maid," "Talking Union," and several others, Seeger beamed, "their applause was deafening."[45]

After the surprise Japanese attack on Pearl Harbor on December 7, 1941, plunged the United States into war, labor songs became less popular. Americans rallied around their flag and unions supported the military effort with no-strike pledges, endorsed by the Communist Party, to ensure that factories operated at full tilt. "I stopped singing 'Talking Union,'" Seeger said. "Made up a new talking blues."[46] This one, sympathetic to the war effort, was called "Dear Mr. President."

Though the Almanac Singers shifted political direction, they could not help but stir the political pot. On their CIO tour, an FBI informant cited their use of crowd psychology to entice audiences into singing left-wing union songs. The FBI took note and filed all *Daily Worker* clippings about both Seeger and the group. Around the time the Almanac Singers sang patriotic beat-Hitler songs on a radio program called *This Is War,* the FBI discovered their highly critical *Songs for John Doe* recording. Within days, newspaper head-lines, like one in the *World-Telegram,* announced, "Singers on New Morale Show Also Warbled for Communists."[47] Though the United States and the Soviet Union were now allies, the charge of abetting Communists destroyed any commercial possibilities for the group.

The Almanac Singers had other problems as well. Different members sang at different events, and sometimes the group appeared, and was, disorganized. It was not always clear who would show up at a booking.

Meanwhile, Seeger fell in love. "I was always pretty shy with girls," he later recalled. "Never really had a steady girlfriend. Tried to a couple times, failed completely." Then he met Toshi Ohta, an attractive young woman with long black hair, a Virginian mother, and a Japanese father. Seeger first encountered her in New York in 1939 and was intrigued by her background and her progressive sympathies. But he was involved in meeting musi-cians and trying to promote the Almanac Singers, and things drifted for a time. In early 1942, Toshi volunteered to help cata-logue song files for the Almanac Singers. "And for a week or two," Seeger said, "I had to walk her home every night because her mother said...don't walk across...Washington Square Park all by yourself at night. So I walked her home and pretty soon we were going steady."[48]

The U.S. Army drafted Seeger and he entered the service in July 1942. As he reported for duty, Toshi told him, "I'll wait for you." Because of his radical background he was not immediately sent overseas: "Military intelligence started investigating me and I stayed in...Mississippi for six months picking up cigarette butts while the rest of my outfit went on to glory and death. I said,

'Toshi, it looks like I'm just going to stay here. We might as well live off the post. Let's get married.'"[49]

The wedding took place at a church in Greenwich Village in New York, when Seeger was on furlough. He had no money for a wedding ring, so Toshi provided the one belonging to her grandmother and paid for the marriage license as well.[50] Almost immediately military authorities decided to keep "suspected Communists" away from the coasts, and Seeger was transferred to Texas, then to Maryland, until he was finally cleared for service overseas.[51]

Seeger sang his way through his military service, both at home and abroad. In Mississippi, while learning how to disassemble

Wedding picture of Pete and Toshi (Berenice Abbott/Commerce Graphics, Ltd.)

airplane engines, he amused himself by playing his banjo and singing outside the barracks during free time, often attracting listeners and other singers in the process. Seeger described one occasion when a group was playing together in the barracks and the sergeant insisted it was time for lights out: "We adjourned to the latrine, at the end of the building, and started going again."[52]

Stationed in Maryland, he traveled to New York for a recording session and a radio show with Alan Lomax and others. In 1944, the Army shipped him overseas, to Saipan. Responsible for hospital entertainment, he sometimes helped patients recuperate by singing to them and teaching them songs. While hosting other entertainers, he also liked to take out his banjo and play himself. He learned new songs from fellow servicemen and from the native islanders and began to appreciate even more the energy

Pete playing for kids in the South Pacific during World War II (Collection of Pete and Toshi Seeger)

and enthusiasm generated by getting groups of people to sing together. "After the war, I want to organize a very large chorus of untrained voices," he wrote to Toshi, as he dreamed of using music to mobilize workers into collective action.[53]

Bored with military service, he was eager to return home when he learned of the birth of his son, Pietu, in August of that year. It became harder still when he heard by mail that his infant son, born without a gallbladder, had died. He and Toshi dealt with their grief on their own until they could be reunited at the end of the war. "The whole last year has been something of a nightmare," he wrote in April 1945.[54] But by August the bloody conflict was over and, like millions of soldiers, he soon returned to the United States.

Seeger was ready to resume the life he had known before his military service. He had come to believe that songs "can help this world survive."[55] At one level, he understood that songs could simply create a sense of feeling good, as if by association: "If you can cheer yourself up, you can perhaps cheer others up."[56] But songs could also have a larger impact. They could encourage the collective action that could demand and achieve political change. Seeger wanted to use music—his kind of music—to make the world a better place. Above all he wanted to use music to help the growing labor movement achieve its aims of respect for the dignity of working men and women and of pay levels that would allow them to survive and prosper. He dreamed of being in the forefront of workers singing songs that created a sense of common identity. It all seemed possible as he looked forward to the brave new postwar world that lay ahead.

· *Two* ·

"If I Had a Hammer"

∞

Home from the war, Seeger was eager to get on with his life. Though reluctant to see the United States enter the war, he did his part. He endured separation from Toshi that included the birth, and death, of his son. Now, like millions of veterans, he was ready to take up again the things he enjoyed before going overseas. In his case that meant singing, whether alone or with a group, and using music to galvanize the working class. But there was always a tension: Could he remain true to those he cared about most in the face of commercial demands as he tried to earn a living?

Home was different from what it had been when he left for the Pacific. World War II brought a return of economic prosperity as huge military demands jump-started factories into full production. Unemployment all but disappeared. On the foreign front, despite the inevitable tensions involved in working with foreign allies, the major powers fought side by side and managed to defeat the Axis dictators. Though tension flared before the war, Americans and Russians were now on good terms. Indeed, Soviet leader Joseph Stalin had been *Time* magazine's Man of the Year in

1942. There was every reason to hope for continued cooperation and collaboration.

But American workers were edgy. They had won the right to organize into unions and to bargain collectively with management and satisfied many of their most pressing demands. Union membership, which increased dramatically in the 1930s, continued to rise during the war. Wages rose during the struggle, but hardly as fast as corporate profits. As fighting stopped and wage and price controls vanished, some jobs ended and the nation faced a rash of strikes. Worried about their future, workers walked out of factories to demand fair treatment as wage and price controls disappeared. In 1946, some 4.6 million workers marched on picket lines, with the most serious stoppages coming in the railroads and soft-coal mines.

Seeger and his friends wanted to resume their efforts to use songs to bolster a sense of union solidarity. While serving in the Army on Saipan, Seeger spoke about continuing the kind of work the Almanac Singers had begun. He wanted, according to one of those friends, to establish "a loosely knit organization, some structure where people could get together to exchange and print songs."[1] Dreaming expansively, he envisioned a branch in New York and another in Los Angeles, with others in between.

That dream resulted in the creation of People's Songs. Seeger was mustered out of the military in December 1945, and the very next month he presided over a meeting that resulted in the formation of an informal association to encourage the creation and spread of radical protest songs. Based in New York, it included a satellite office in Los Angeles, with other members in even more casual groups in San Francisco and Chicago.

Pete playing at a union meeting (Collection of Pete and Toshi Seeger)

Seeger was the driving force. People's Songs included on its board of directors members of the now defunct Almanac Singers, such as Lee Hays and Woody Guthrie, and later tapped such well-known artists as the radical activist Paul Robeson, who had not been part of the earlier group. But it was Seeger's energy that got the organization off the ground. He served as national director and his vision determined its direction. When asked about his goal in January 1946, he replied, "Make a singing labor movement. Period."[2]

Seeger wanted "to have hundreds, thousands, tens of thousands of union choruses. Just as every church has a choir, why not every union?"[3] He dreamed of bringing singers together to share words and music, of providing access to anyone interested, and encouraging people to sing both the old and new songs he loved. Singing songs in unison could foster a common commitment to work for social and political change. At the same time, the labor movement and its goals remained foremost in his mind; he was convinced that "the revival of interest in folk music would come through the trade unions": "There was the singing tradition of the old IWW [Industrial Workers of the World] to build on. We envisioned a singing labor movement spearheading a nationwide folk music revival."[4]

Seeger helped put out the first issue of the *People's Songs Bulletin* on a mimeograph machine. He recognized that the organization, like the *Bulletin,* was "a shoestring operation" and he understood it required a hands-on effort. The budget was minuscule. Even a salary of $25 a week seemed "extravagant" to Seeger.[5] Despite his optimistic intentions, he tried to be practical about the publication schedule: "I wanted it to be a weekly; others persuaded me to be more conservative and make it a monthly."[6]

The first issue of the *Bulletin* appeared in February 1946. Beneath the masthead it boldly announced its purpose:

The people are on the march and must have songs to sing. Now, in 1946, the truth must reassert itself in many singing voices.

There are thousands of unions, people's organizations, singers, and choruses who would gladly use more songs. There are many songwriters, amateur and professional, who are writing these songs.

It is clear that there must be an organization to make and send songs of labor and the American people through the land.

To do this job, we have formed PEOPLE'S SONGS, INC.

We invite you to join us.[7]

Over the next several years, the *People's Songs Bulletin* included old folk songs like "Tom Dooley" and "Big Rock Candy Mountain," along with a number of Woody Guthrie's playful "Songs to Grow On." It carried uplifting songs like Guthrie's "Roll On, Columbia," in praise of New Deal public power projects in the Pacific Northwest. But it also printed hard-hitting labor songs—"Eight Hours," "UAW-CIO," "Capitalistic Boss," and "The Scabs Crawl In"—that highlighted the difficult conditions workers still faced in their factory jobs.[8]

The *Bulletin* also provided occasional commentary on the folk music scene. The singer Cisco Houston wrote about the songs he sang during his wartime experience onboard ship, and Lee Hays recounted his efforts at staging folklore performances during his early teaching career. Those involved in the operation applauded the modest magazine and were heartened as the *Bulletin* gained a thousand subscribers in its first year, before circulation leveled off.

In those first few years after the war, People's Songs participants were optimistic about what they could accomplish. "One dreams of a great people's song," Lee Hays wrote, "of our marching song which will come again but hasn't yet; of the great song which is still unsung. It will be a hymn, for it will be born in faith, and love, and united purpose. It will be a battle hymn, for we are at war against the powers of evil."[9] Members believed that their efforts could expose injustice, and, like many reformers, they assumed that knowledge would prompt action to make the world a better place.

Seeger, once the observer and now the activist, seemed to be everywhere. In addition to directing the People's Songs organization and editing the *Bulletin,* he gave talks at conferences on folklore, composed songs and taught others how to write them, and organized People's Songs "hootenannies" to raise money for mimeographing costs and rent.

Hootenannies were gatherings in a hall or a house to sing songs. Guthrie and Seeger had seen people singing in unison in Seattle in 1941, the crescendo of sound lifting spirits and creating a sense of solidarity. Members of the Washington Commonwealth Federation, a New Deal club, had arranged for the two visitors to sing at a number of trade unions, Seeger recalled: "Then [they] proudly invited us to their next 'hootenanny.' It was the first time we had heard the term. It seems they had a vote to decide what they would call their monthly fund-raising parties. 'Hootenanny' won out by a nose over 'wingding.'" Seeger was impressed with what he saw. "The Seattle hootenannies were real community affairs," he said approvingly. "One family would bring a huge pot of some dish like crab gumbo. Others would bring cakes, salads. A drama group performed topical skits, a good 16-mm film might be shown, and there would be dancing, swing and folk, for those of sound limb. And, of course, there would be singing."[10]

The Almanac Singers held hootenannies before the war. Now those involved with People's Songs revived them. The first New York hootenanny took place at the home of the Ohtas, Seeger's in-laws, and attracted eighty people. Then 112 showed up at a second in an apartment on Thompson Street and 300 at a third at the Newspaper Guild hall in New York. In April 1946, one thousand people came to a gathering with twenty performers at Irving Plaza. Describing the last session, *Time* magazine reported, "The lyrics were black and white (and sometimes red) versions of current events. The result was not always good singing or good logic."[11] Woody Guthrie reacted more effusively: "I saw these People's Songs raise up storms of stiff winds and wild howls of cheer from the people in their seats, and saw also, that almost every chronic headache was eased and made quieter."[12] For the participants, at least, a hootenanny created a giddy atmosphere.

Seeger had his own ideas about what made these gatherings work: "The best hoot, in my opinion, would have an audience of several hundred, jammed tight into a small hall, and seated semicircularwise, so that they face each other democratically." He loved having all kinds of singers and musicians, amateur and professional, young and old, singing alongside each other.

Singing and playing in a crowd in the 1940s (Collection of Pete and Toshi Seeger)

"Some songs might be quiet—like a pin drop. Others would shake the floor and rafters until the nails loosen. Something old and something new, something borrowed and something blue, as at a wedding."[13]

Seeger moved ahead in all directions. He and his associates organized a song library and made songs available through songbooks, sheet music, records, and, of course, the *People's Songs Bulletin*. Membership in People's Songs reached two thousand. Famous folksingers like Burl Ives and Josh White gave their support to People's Songs activities. In August 1946 the *New York Times* reported encouragingly, "People's Songs keeps a musical stethoscope on the heartbeat of the nation, translating current events into notes and lyrics."[14]

As members of the new organization forged ahead, many remained sympathetic to Communist Party support for working men and women. Some of the People's Songs activists were Party members; others were not. Seeger himself "somehow joined the cultural section of the Party."[15] He was more concerned with using his talents to communicate with ordinary people than with clinging to doctrinaire political positions.

Although party leaders considered music irrelevant to the class struggle, some active in left-wing politics viewed the new group more positively. The author Michael Gold, writing in the Communist *Daily Worker*, noted in early 1946, "I will report the little fact that a group of former Almanac Singers, plus others concerned with labor music, started to organize something again the day before New Year. Songs, songs of, by and for the people! ... The spirit has not died—it has only been unemployed."[16] Communist connections helped build audiences but also aroused suspicion and sometimes hostility in the face of growing anti-Communist sentiment.

As 1946 unfolded, American attitudes toward the Soviet Union hardened. Disagreements over what kind of government would rule in Poland and other parts of Eastern Europe eroded the remnants of wartime goodwill. In February Stalin lashed out at the Western powers, proclaiming his confidence that Communism would triumph over capitalism. In March, with President Harry Truman looking on approvingly, former British prime minister Winston Churchill declared, "An iron curtain has descended across the continent."[17] A new war, soon christened the "Cold War," was under way.

Domestic politics reflected international polarization. Continuing strikes caused frustration on the part of inconvenienced consumers who wanted to get their hands on anything and everything after the deprivations of depression and war. Responding to disruptions, Republicans were determined to regain control of Congress in the midterm elections of 1946 and to strike a blow against the Democrat Truman, who seemed a poor substitute for FDR. Truman's support, which had stood at 87 percent when he became president in 1945, dropped to 32 percent at election time. Truman and the Democratic Party were particularly vulnerable on labor issues in the face of Republican attacks that New Deal support had made unions too strong.

In that setting the members of People's Songs plunged into the 1946 elections. They worked largely with the Political Action Committee (PAC) of the CIO in the effort to send to Congress progressive representatives sympathetic to labor. Some of them wrote and recorded jingles about housing, inflation, and other issues that could be used to support a variety of candidates. In September, Seeger and others recorded an album for the campaign called *Songs for Political Action*. It featured such titles as "A Dollar Ain't a Dollar Anymore" and "No, No, No Discrimination."[18]

Democrats fared abysmally in the elections. Republicans asked "Had enough?" and voters responded "Yes!" When the votes were counted, Republicans controlled both houses of Congress for the first time since 1928 and won a majority of governorships as well.

Republican victories helped fuel a growing anti-Communist movement in the United States. Republicans charged that a Democratic willingness to work closely with the Soviet Union during and after the war endangered American security and stability. The charge, though unfair, stuck.

Old legislation was now mustered into the service of the new anti-Communist crusade. The Smith Act, passed in 1940, made it a crime to advocate the forcible overthrow of the United States, and Communism, with its confidence in the inevitable demise of capitalism and the triumph of a classless society, was now suspect.

Communists who held positions of responsibility in some CIO unions also faced the wrath of the new Republican-controlled Congress. The Taft-Hartley Act, passed by Congress in 1947 over Truman's veto, restricted union activities and required union officials to sign oaths swearing that they were not Communists. In that climate, People's Songs, with its Communist connections and active support for the CIO, encountered hard times.

Trouble began when the House Un-American Activities Committee (HUAC), which had investigated fascism during the war, focused on Communist subversion in the United States. In

1945, it became a permanent standing committee, relying on a close association with the FBI and J. Edgar Hoover, its virulently anti-Communist director. As soon as People's Songs set up its office in New York, the FBI opened a file on the organization.

Seeger and his colleagues came under attack. *Broadcasting,* a newsletter for the radio industry, used material provided by HUAC to characterize them as former "members of the Young Communist League, and of the Almanac Singers."[19] The journalist Frederick Woltman relied on similar information to warn readers of the *New York World-Telegram,* "The lyrical Leftists have been furnishing their propaganda-with-music to Communist and Red-front affairs until CIO-PAC decided to give them a national audience."[20]

In the face of mounting criticism of People's Songs, members of the group tried to keep the charges in perspective. Woody Guthrie described the criticism as politically motivated Red-baiting. A report about the smear tactics to the national board suggested, perhaps too optimistically, "Because of their obvious red-herring technique content, these articles do not particularly harm People's Songs."[21]

Ignoring hostile comments, the loose-knit group pushed ahead. Leaders sought to establish a respectable veneer by enlisting the support of such musical luminaries as Aaron Copland, Leonard Bernstein, and Oscar Hammerstein II. Their names now appeared on the *Bulletin*'s masthead, although they played no role in the everyday work of the organization. Meanwhile volunteers worked in the one-room office, transcribing songs, managing files, maintaining a library, and talking on the telephone to make sure musicians were paid.

In mid-1947, Irwin Silber, a recent graduate of Brooklyn College, took over as executive secretary of People's Songs and helped the group shape up. Seeger still remained the heart of the organization, but Silber helped it run smoothly.

Seeger welcomed organizational assistance, for he was busier than ever. Despite the birth of another son, he was in and out of his house "like a boarder." He was trying to do everything at once: "I felt shot through with adrenalin as I dashed around from appointment to appointment. Just think of getting so much done in a short time!...Poor Toshi. She stayed home changing diapers and I'd get home at one A.M. from one committee meeting, then be off at seven the next morning to another."[22] It was difficult for Toshi, who took care of the children largely by herself.

Even as he focused his efforts on People's Songs, Seeger was making a name for himself as a solo singer. He did a stint at the Village Vanguard in New York and received good reviews in the press. The trade journal *Billboard* called him "the trim, slim Sinatra of the folksong clan," and the highbrow *New Yorker* described his singing as "fresh" and "contagious."[23]

The different strands of Seeger's life came together in the fall of 1947, when People's Songs put on its first national convention, called Sing Out, America. It took place in Chicago, in Hull House, the social settlement established by the reformer Jane Addams at the end of the nineteenth century. Several dozen delegates participated in workshops, talked about organizational details, held a square dance, and put on a public hootenanny that drew more than two thousand participants. "Running through all the debate, disagreement, fun...was a serious note of purpose," Silber observed. "This was no businessman's convention, but a gathering of people who are afraid for their country and its democratic heritage—and who are determined to chart a path for people's music in the gigantic struggles looming up ahead."[24]

The FBI took careful note of the convention. At least one agent was present and reported that "the program had a definite 'pinkish tinge.'"[25] Over the next several years, the FBI continued its investigation of People's Songs, tapping phones, collecting documents, and infiltrating meetings.

The FBI had no trouble finding material, for in 1948 Seeger and People's Songs moved into partisan politics. President Truman faced a reelection challenge from Henry A. Wallace, FDR's former vice president and subsequently secretary of commerce. Truman had fired Wallace from the Cabinet for being too sympathetic to the Soviet Union. Wallace mounted a presidential campaign of his own on a Progressive Party ticket. Radicals thought that Wallace, far more than the unpopular Truman or the Republican candidate Thomas A. Dewey, represented the future. Not only did Wallace attract show business luminaries like Paul Robeson and Harry Belafonte, but he also garnered strong Communist Party support.

People's Songs stood squarely behind Wallace, and Seeger embraced the cause with optimism. He sang at the Progressive Party convention in Philadelphia that nominated Wallace and at a large Wallace rally in Yankee Stadium in New York. Along with Paul Robeson he toured with the candidate, sometimes bringing Toshi and Mika, their new baby, to campaign events.

Some of the campaigning was fun, but there was often tension in the air. Wallace favored civil rights reform and an end to

Campaigning with Henry Wallace (Collection of Pete and Toshi Seeger)

segregation more strongly than his opponents did and frequently faced the ire not just of the Ku Klux Klan but of conservative white Americans with more rigid racial views. Songs, Seeger felt, might soften the antagonism: "I think it [singing] probably helped prevent people from getting killed. It was a very touch and go proposition, that tour."[26]

One disappointment for Seeger was the lack of labor support for Wallace. Recognizing political realities, union leaders understood that Truman could better serve their interests, and after passage of the Taft-Hartley Act, which restricted union activity, they were reluctant to associate themselves too closely with the Communist cause. Seeger, whose own sympathies always lay with working men and women, found himself in a bind but believed that Wallace was his only choice. And so People's Songs focused on the campaign and derived what income it could from its Progressive Party bookings. In the end, those efforts made little difference. Drawing only a million votes, Wallace finished fourth, behind Truman, Dewey, and the segregationist candidate Strom Thurmond.

Even worse, People's Songs was falling into bankruptcy. The organization owed back salaries and had run up debts of $2,000 in the first year, $8,000 in the second, and had come to owe close to $12,000, a sizable sum in 1949.[27] Early in the year, unable to come up with the money to pay landlords and printers, it closed its doors. The next year many of the same people who had worked with People's Songs established a new magazine, *Sing Out!*, which took a less aggressively political approach. It managed to stay afloat, and in that way kept the singing tradition alive.

People's Songs was gone, and Seeger mourned its loss. "Looking over the pages of the little mimeographed bulletin of 1946," he observed a dozen years later, "I am at times appalled by its amateurishness, and at other times filled with a flush of pride for the bravery and honesty. Maybe fools walk in where angels fear to tread, but here's to the young and foolish, and may the world have more of them."[28] For all of the exuberance, the organization died because of its "failure to get unions to sing." At that point Pete and his colleagues "didn't know how to write songs that would catch on."[29]

Disappointed by the demise of People's Songs, Seeger decided to leave New York City as well. "By 1949," he said, "I could see the disadvantages of city life. My health wasn't any good. I got no exercise except by running up and down stairs. Each day was a list of phone calls a foot long."[30] It all made him tired. "I wanted to think about music a little more and not be under pressure to be at a committee meeting every hour on the hour, every day in the week, which is what my life in New York had become."[31]

Tarnished by his association with the Wallace campaign as the anti-Communist crusade gained strength, he sometimes found commercial bookings scarce. To a friend he commented, "I guess I ought to think about getting a job in a factory."[32] Instead he and Toshi borrowed money from friends and relatives in the spring of 1949 and bought seventeen and a half acres of land overlooking the Hudson River near Beacon, about an hour and half north of the city. Always fond of the outdoors, Seeger planned to chop wood, trim logs, and build a cabin for the family with his own hands.

That summer, living in a tent or sometimes in a small trailer, Pete and Toshi cleared the land. Then he went to the New York Public Library to find instructions on how to build a log cabin. By fall he had cut the necessary logs and dug the foundation. A year later, he recalled, "We had the walls and the roof on and the windows and doors in. It wasn't much fixed up, but it was a house."[33]

Seeger still had occasional invitations to perform and had begun to sing with a new group. A year before, he had written and mimeographed a small instructional manual, *How to Play the 5-String Banjo,* but sales were sparse and few royalties came in. It was a struggle to survive. Still, Toshi later recalled, "I never felt poor" coming out of the Depression, when everyone had a hard time.[34]

Poor or not, Seeger was always ready to sing for a good cause. In September 1949 an opportunity arose. He was invited to par-

The cabin in Beacon during construction (Collection of Pete and Toshi Seeger)

ticipate in a concert featuring Paul Robeson in Peekskill, New York, just north of New York City on the Hudson River. The aim was to raise money for the Communist Party's civil rights wing. Though Seeger had drifted away from the Party, he remained sympathetic to its purposes.[35] The baritone Robeson had a sparkling musical reputation that complemented his left-wing political stance. He reflected the energy of the black community and radical hopes for resisting persecution and creating a social base for an energetic protest movement. Irwin Silber noted, "He was, for us, the quintessential role model of the committed artist."[36]

Peekskill, reputedly a center of Ku Klux Klan activity, posed problems. A week or so earlier, another concert had run into resistance. Approaching the venue then, Seeger had hailed a state trooper: "I'm one of the performers tonight—can you help me get through?" The officer replied, "The concert has been called off. It's impossible for anyone to get through."[37]

Seeger later learned that the American Legion, yelling "dirty Commie" and "dirty kike," had destroyed concert equipment and beaten the people preparing the stage.[38] Robeson and other organizers refused to be intimidated and rescheduled the event.

This time the concert took place. Three hundred demonstrators yelled that the musicians should "go back to Russia" and bellowed such obscenities as "nigger-lovers." A line of union members, standing shoulder to shoulder around the open field with the stage at the center, kept the intruders from getting close.[39] An audience of twenty-five thousand heard Seeger perform a few selections before Robeson sang "Ol' Man River," a song he had made famous, and other numbers. The concert ended early so that people could get away before dark.

As soon as the singing was over Seeger and the other performers "congratulated ourselves that things had gone smoothly." They spoke too soon. As the cars snaked out of the field a policeman directed all traffic down a single narrow road.

The reason became clear when Seeger saw broken glass on the road and realized that men with handfuls of rocks were hurling

Peekskill riot car (Collection of Pete and Toshi Seeger)

them at the passing cars. Pete spied a policeman just ahead and asked for help, only to be told by the angry officer, "Move on! Keep moving!"[40] Over the next two miles, ten to fifteen rocks hit the car, smashing nearly every window. Seeger's three-year-old son, Danny, crouched underneath his mother but was still covered with glass. Policemen looked on with approval.[41]

The Peekskill riot was not a spontaneous uprising but a carefully orchestrated attack arranged by the Ku Klux Klan and the local police. Lee Hays wondered about the blind fury that prompted the violence: "What is there in the music of Chopin, Bartók, Mendelssohn, and in the people's songs of Paul Robeson and Pete Seeger...to inspire this savagery, this hatred? Who but beasts are menaced by a culture which brings people together in peace and understanding?"[42] The answer was simple: those who feared change and hated African Americans as much as they hated Communists.

Seeger wondered what would happen next. He had begun to sing with a new group, a quartet that included Hays and sought to be a more polished and better rehearsed version of the Almanac Singers. The other two members, both a bit younger, were Fred Hellerman and Ronnie Gilbert. Hellerman, a recent Brooklyn College graduate, had learned to play the guitar in the Coast Guard and spent time in the People's Songs office. Gilbert was a voice student whose mother, a member of the International Ladies Garment Workers Union, introduced her young daughter to labor politics through the Wobblies' songbook. Hellerman's baritone voice and Gilbert's alto mingled beautifully with Seeger's tenor and Hays's bass to create an unusually pleasing sound.

The four musicians began singing together on Wednesday afternoons in the Ohtas' home in New York, at People's Songs hootenannies, and then at other radical gatherings in early 1949. The group also performed as the No-Name Quartet on a weekly folk music program hosted by the singer Oscar Brand on radio station WNYC. The quartet finally settled on the Weavers. The name was drawn from a play by the German author Gerhart Hauptmann that dealt with defiant weavers in medieval England.[43] Though its origins were obscure the name suited the group perfectly, for it reflected musical harmonies woven together seamlessly.

The Weavers. From left to right: Pete, Lee Hays, Ronnie Gilbert, and Fred Hellerman (Collection of Pete and Toshi Seeger)

As the Weavers searched for old songs, they also composed new ones. Hays, the son of a Methodist minister, had been raised on hymns and liked the old gospel pattern of changing just one word in each successive verse. He began to play with an idea and in no time at all had three verses, then a fourth to tie the others together. In January 1949, he sent what he had to Seeger and asked him to come up with a melody. Banging out notes on a piano,

Seeger soon had the music, not "a bad tune, but it wasn't as good as it should be."[44] "If I Had a Hammer" turned out to be better than Seeger ever imagined.

The Weavers recorded the song on Charter Records later that year. "If I Had a Hammer" soon graced the cover of the first issue of *Sing Out!*, the publication that took the place of the defunct *People's Songs Bulletin*. It began:

> If I had a hammer
> I'd hammer in the morning,
> I'd hammer in the evening,
> All over this land;
> I'd hammer out danger,
> I'd hammer out a warning,
> I'd hammer out love between
> All of my brothers
> All over this land.

The second and third verses followed the same format, only this time beginning "If I had a bell" and then "If I had a song." The final verse pulled all of the elements together:

> Well, I got a hammer,
> And I got a bell,
> And I got a song
> All over this land;
> It's the hammer of justice,
> It's the bell of freedom;
> It's a song about love between all of my brothers
> All over this land.[45]

The song had a driving beat, repetitive elements that made it easy to remember, and, despite Seeger's skepticism, a catchy tune.

Conservative critics complained that it counseled radical, and hence unacceptable, activism. Worse still, the hammer seemed painfully close to the hammer that appeared along with a sickle on the Soviet flag.

As they performed the song, the Weavers themselves debated whether the lyrics should be altered. At one concert, a woman suggested changing "love between all of my brothers" to "love between my brothers and my sisters." Hays balked, arguing that the original phrase flowed better off the tongue. How about "all of my siblings," he quipped with his own tongue planted heavily in his cheek. Criticisms notwithstanding, the Weavers stuck with their original wording in most early renditions of the song.[46] Although audiences liked it, Seeger later joked that the record became a collector's item, for only a collector would have a copy.

Despite the record and occasional performances, the singers had trouble making ends meet. The Peekskill riot had a chilling effect on audiences, and some members of the group wanted to disband. Seeger still hoped the Weavers would find a following. He suggested that the owner of the Village Vanguard, a club featuring live music in Greenwich Village, might book the Weavers for the same fee he had once paid Seeger as a solo act. "Rather than go there by myself," he proposed, "let's go in as a group. If we split my salary four ways, we'd each get fifty dollars a week."[47] In need of money, Seeger was determined to have the group succeed: "I decided to stop congratulating myself on not going commercial."[48]

The Weavers opened at the Village Vanguard during Christmas week in 1949. They stayed for six months. Though audiences dwindled, the owner, Max Gordon, admired Seeger and allowed the group to continue. Beginning with Christmas carols at their

"The Hammer Song" in the very first issue of Sing Out! (© The Sing Out! Corporation, all rights reserved)

opening, they were soon singing a variety of folk songs, trying out different harmonies and making many traditional songs better known in the process. One night Alan Lomax brought Carl Sandburg to hear them. "When I hear America singing, the Weavers are there," the great poet declared. "[They are] out of the grass roots of America. I salute them."[49]

As the Weavers gained popularity, Seeger realized that they needed a manager. Harold Leventhal, progressive politically, active in show business, and a fellow worker in the Wallace campaign, first suggested a friend and later ended up representing the group himself. The Weavers signed a recording contract with Decca Records, a major label whose executives were taken with their knack for making music accessible to the public.

Their first record had the Israeli song "Tzena, Tzena, Tzena" on one side and Lead Belly's "Goodnight, Irene" on the other. Orchestrated by the bandleader Gordon Jenkins, who worked for Decca, the musical accompaniment for "Goodnight, Irene" included a chorus and violins. Even though the Weavers used only Seeger's banjo and Hellerman's guitar in performances, Seeger tolerated the orchestration. He was willing to do almost anything to "make a dent in the wall that seemed to be between [the Weavers] and the American people."[50] He even donned a tuxedo for concerts.

Both songs were hits. One followed the other to the top of the charts, even though disc jockeys were not sure at first whether they belonged on country or pop lists. Other hits followed: "On Top of Old Smoky," "Kisses Sweeter Than Wine," and a new version that Woody Guthrie wrote of his classic Dust Bowl ballad,

"So Long, It's Been Good to Know You." Over a two-year period Decca sold four million Weavers records.[51]

Critical acclaim came along with commercial success. In the summer of 1951 *Newsweek* wrote, "Just a year and a half ago, the Weavers burst upon the New York scene in a tiny Greenwich Village night club called the Village Vanguard. Since then, they have toured the country and their salaries have zoomed from $200 to $4,000 a week."[52] The next month, *Time* reported that "a group of four high-spirited folksters known as the Weavers had succeeded in shouting, twanging and crooning folk singing out of its cloistered corner into the commercial big time."[53]

Seeger kept the Weavers going. Hays later hailed his colleague's talent and experience and collection of songs, enough to keep the quartet in business for years.[54]

But Seeger suffered on the road. He was lonely, especially when the group was touring and performing in clubs, theaters, and hotels on the West Coast for six months. Toshi left their two children, ages two and four, with her parents and joined him in what she later called "the worst thing I ever did in my life."[55] Her presence helped, but they both missed the children. Everywhere he went Pete took out photographs of the children and put them under the glass top of the hotel room dresser.[56]

It was also difficult to see old friends from People's Songs and other radical organizations. They felt the Weavers had abandoned their principles by becoming commercially successful and popular. Seeger himself was not comfortable in a tuxedo and sometimes wore red socks in silent protest.[57] He wasn't happy when told by an early manager not to sing at political events or even to record "If I Had a Hammer" for commercial distribution.

Although he had abandoned the Communist Party at about the time the Weavers got together, he was still committed to left-wing causes. On occasion, he snuck out to attend meetings of radical groups in cities where the Weavers were performing.

Earning a good living by doing what he loved helped ease his ambivalence. So did the sound of his voice coming from a record store as he walked by. A broad smile would turn the edges of his mouth upward, and he would laugh out loud with delight.[58] Greater satisfaction came from creating the kind of singing movement he had been hoping to spark for years.

Union songs had never achieved much popularity in the 1940s. Now the Weavers were reviving traditional tunes, introducing melodies from around the world, popularizing some of Woody Guthrie's and Lead Belly's best contributions, all the while promoting the values of racial and ethnic harmony and brotherhood. They were breaking down the often artificial boundaries between different kinds of music. As their songs soared on the charts, they helped make folk music acceptable to everyone's tastes. Seeger was not building the kind of singing labor movement he had sought earlier, but he and his fellow musicians were making Americans aware of their musical past. With their pleasing harmonies and lively sound, the Weavers were building a new audience ready to ignite a huge folk music revival in the decades ahead.

· *Three* ·

"Where Have All the Flowers Gone?"

∞

Seeger didn't see it coming. Everything was going so well—the music, the bookings, the marriage to Toshi, which now boasted two healthy children. The Weavers were at the height of their popularity, making more money and hammering out more songs than ever. Suddenly, like a clap of thunder on a sunny day, their bubble burst. They were the ones being hammered. A Red Scare more destructive than the one that followed World War I left them reeling under charges of being Communist subversives.

The attacks came just as the Weavers were beginning to relish their success. They were appealing to mainstream America with enviable results. *Time* magazine called the foursome "the most imitated group in the business."[1] Listeners loved the melodies and harmonies of their songs, some of them songs they had sung as children, songs that captured the folk roots of American life. They bought records, lots of them, and flocked to concerts all over the country.

As the Weavers enjoyed the experience of making good money for the first time, they faced a nightmare they couldn't ignore. Anyone sympathetic to the Soviet Union, in the present or the past, was suspect. Seeger, like his father, had Communist connections. After all, he sympathized openly with Communism's egalitarian goals, he read the *Daily Worker,* and he had even been a formal member of the Party for a time.

Anyone with Communist connections came under attack in America's second Red Scare. As relations between the United States and the Soviet Union chilled after World War II, it seemed as if the whole world was turning red. Much of Eastern Europe soon found itself under Soviet domination. In Greece, Turkey, Italy, and France, Communists threatened peace and stability, even threatened to take over. China fell to the Communists in 1949, and in 1950 Communist North Korea attacked South Korea, igniting a war that quickly drew in the United States.

The rising red tide abroad inflamed anxieties about reds at home. A series of spectacular spy cases fed fears that somehow Communists were infiltrating the United States, threatening the very foundations of American society. Subversion, real and imagined, had to be rooted out wherever it appeared. Those who had flirted with radical causes in the 1930s, when capitalism seemed on the edge of destruction, now faced accusations of disloyalty. Those who, like Seeger, joined the Communist Party at any point in their lives came under suspicion.

The crusade to root out Communism took different forms. President Truman established the Federal Employee Loyalty Program in 1947, aimed at identifying government employees who might be security risks. Meanwhile Congress embarked on its own investigations, largely through HUAC. Working with reports from FBI informers and investigating other allegations, the committee demanded that people testify about their political past or face criminal charges. "Are you now or have you ever been a member of the Communist Party?" was a question that reverberated through hearing rooms.[2] Even if the Loyalty Program or HUAC produced no formal charges, a person could be ruined by a whisper here or a rumor there. Such was the power of fear that the merest hint of association with radical causes or with people suspected of associating with radical causes could end a career or a line of credit or even a lifetime friendship.

Seeger became a target. The fact that he left the Party made no difference; prior associations counted as much as current ones. HUAC demanded that people divulge details about their own experiences and those of their associates at the time and earlier. Toward the end of June 1950, a vitriolic anti-Communist booklet, *Red Channels: The Report of Communist Influence in Radio and Television,* listed the allegedly compromising left-wing activities of numerous well-known entertainers. Published by the right-wing journal *Counterattack,* a self-professed *Newsletter of Facts to Combat Communism, Red Channels* relied on *Daily Worker* clippings and related published materials in FBI files to challenge the loyalty of a broad spectrum of men and women working in radio, television, and film. Pete Seeger's name appeared in *Red Channels* thirteen times.[3]

As the anti-Communist crusade gained momentum, the Weavers tried to move carefully. Pete Kameron, an early manager, continued to bend over backward to keep Seeger from singing at radical gatherings. He was even more insistent that Seeger change his image.

Seeger was mystified. "I don't see what's wrong," he said. "I've always sung at hoots." Kameron refused to back down: "Now isn't the time. You don't want to jeopardize the position you're in."[4]

Politics affected performance. On one occasion Seeger suggested that the Weavers sing "If I Had a Hammer" in concert. Mindful of the climate of suspicion, the others demurred. "Oh, no," one of them said. "We can't get away with anything like that."[5]

As Seeger thought about the powerful song and its message, he wondered, "Why was it controversial?" What was happening to the country? "In 1949, only 'Commies' used words like 'peace' and 'freedom.'"[6] Somehow that usage contaminated innocent terminology. The more he thought about it, the more puzzling it became, for the message was clearly upbeat: "This is what a lot of spirituals say. We *will* overcome. I *have* a hammer. The last verse didn't say 'well, I guess there is no hammer, I guess there is no bell, I guess there is no song, so honey, let's forget it and have a good time.' We could have said that....But the last verse says 'I *have* a hammer, I *have* a bell, I *have* a song.' Here it is. 'It's the hammer of justice, it's the bell of freedom, the song of love.'"[7] He was right, of course, but the quartet refused to sing the song nonetheless.

For a time, the Weavers managed to avoid a confrontation with anti-Communists. Despite the publicity about Seeger's radical past, the group's songs remained at the top of the pop charts and the Weavers remained in demand. Finally, in the summer of 1951, the Red-baiting crusade caught up with them. A scheduled spot on Dave Garroway's television variety show inexplicably disappeared. Though they had been on the program for a public appearance at the Ohio State Fair, the governor responded to the hostile publicity by demanding successfully that the invitation be withdrawn.

Things grew worse in February 1952, when an FBI informer, Harvey Matusow, testified before HUAC about the Weavers' Communist connections. Matusow had earlier offered to help sell records for People's Songs before the organization went bankrupt. Under oath before HUAC, he claimed that all of the Weavers, with the exception of Lee Hays, were members of the Communist Party. Weeks later, he elaborated on his allegations before the Ohio Un-American Activities Commission: "[The Weavers' popularity] was used to attract many young people to the movement because they respected the Weavers and thought they were good singers and entertainers. The bobbysoxers go for that. Once the young people were at the affair, the Communist Party organizer took over. He had a good chance to recruit many of the young people."[8]

Like other entertainers under attack, the Weavers soon found themselves victims of a blacklist. People appearing on such a list could not find work, for employers refused to hire them, and many careers ground to an end. "We had started off singing in some very flossy nightclubs," Seeger said. They had been welcome at fancy establishments like the Palmer House in Chicago. "Then we went lower and lower as the blacklist crowded us in. Finally, we were down to places like Daffy's Bar and Grill on the outskirts of Cleveland."[9]

Fans and fellow singers could not miss what was happening. *Variety,* the entertainment magazine, observed that the foursome was "the first group canceled out of a New York café because of alleged left-wing affiliations."[10] *Downbeat,* the bible of musical performance, noted the absurdity of trying to deal with the ban the Weavers faced: "If the Communists happen to come out in favor of milk for babies, go on record immediately as being squarely opposed to it."[11] Kameron went to *Counterattack* to get the magazine to retract its charges, but to no avail.

The Weavers were in trouble. "We kept on with personal appearances," Seeger said, "but it got to be more and more of a drag."[12] It became almost futile to continue. "Very quickly our work came down to nothing, there was no work to be had," Ronnie Gilbert moaned.[13] Following an annual concert at Town Hall in New York City in December 1952, the group disbanded. The singers took a sabbatical that, according to Lee Hays, "turned into a Mondayical and Tuesdayical."[14]

Three years later the Weavers held a reunion concert. It was a gamble: the Red Scare had not yet subsided and HUAC was still summoning witnesses to testify about their past. But change was in the air. Senator Joseph R. McCarthy, a focal figure in the anti-Communist crusade, pushed too hard in his insistence that the Army was harboring subversives, and the public, after weeks of televised hearings, wearied of his attacks.

Harold Leventhal, now in charge of Seeger's career, thought there might be a possibility of challenging the blacklist with a public concert. He made the necessary arrangements and told the singers they were going to perform. He wanted to return to Town Hall, the scene of their final concert, but the anxious proprietors refused his request. Leventhal turned instead to Carnegie Hall. Though this stage normally featured classical music concerts, those in charge needed cash and agreed to the rental deal without knowing too much about the Weavers.

The concert sold out immediately and 2,800 undaunted fans filled the hall. "The air was charged as at few concerts," according to the music critic Robert Shelton. "The fans had returned in multitudes, and the group's electrical rapport with its admirers was fully reestablished."[15] Leventhal recorded the concert, and the record *The Weavers at Carnegie Hall* appeared in 1957 on the Vanguard label. The Weavers began to tour again, mostly on the weekends, and continued to record for Vanguard. Seeger, who had tired of the travel and wearied of singing the same songs night after night, left the group in 1957, but the Weavers continued to tour and record with a replacement.

Pete singing alone with his banjo (Collection of Pete and Toshi Seeger)

Seeger resumed performing solo. Always dedicated to making folk music available, he wanted to find his own voice. Ignoring regular concert halls, Pete and Toshi decided that he would make a living singing in colleges, churches, summer camps, and schools. Those venues offered him a different audience from those he had known, one not always knowledgeable about folk music but eager to listen and learn. The challenge was exciting.

Seeger was comfortable with his choice. His experience with the pop music world persuaded him that he needed something different: "I didn't want a commercial career. I looked upon nightclubs as foolish places where people got drunk. People went away to forget their troubles. I wanted to see if we could solve our troubles with my songs. I didn't want people to forget their

Pete performing in a school auditorium (Collection of Pete and Toshi Seeger)

troubles."[16] With his wife's help he put together a brochure advertising his availability, and Toshi took care of bookings.

It was grueling. Because Pete had to travel to sing, he was often on the road. He had always been busy, and engagements with the Weavers had taken him away from his cabin on the Hudson. But now his schedule became even more hectic. He was lucky that Toshi was willing to stay home to care for the children, and she did so without complaint. It wasn't easy living alone in the woods without electricity or other creature comforts. Toshi avoided dwelling on it for I "would have been scared out of my wits."[17] Thinking later about the effect of his musical and political activities on his family life, Seeger acknowledged, "It was a real case of the male supremacist organizer who expects the wife to run the house while he's changing the world."[18]

Slowly Seeger began to build a following. He had no choice but to start at the grass roots. He traveled to schools and summer camps, accepting bookings for $25 or $50. Eventually he began to visit college campuses. As his friend and fellow singer Don McLean pointed out, "The blacklist was the best thing that ever happened to him; it forced him into a situation of struggle, which he thrived on."[19]

Despite the hardships, Seeger remained optimistic. The upbeat attitude was part of his nature. When faced with difficulty, he took things one step at a time, relying on his music to keep him going without complaint. He felt like Johnny Appleseed, the great American folk hero. Born John Chapman around the time of the American Revolution, he had gone to Harvard and moved on, like Pete, roaming the wilderness, giving farmers seeds to plant in return for lodging. Seeger began to write about Johnny Appleseed in a new column that regularly appeared in *Sing Out!:* "Many thought him eccentric, thousands loved him, but all recognized the practicality of his system." Pete hoped the same might be said of him one day.[20]

As he brought America's songs to new audiences, Seeger perfected his own musical style. By now a master of his musical instrument, he could make his banjo sing and used it to get audiences to join him. People accustomed to sitting quietly or perhaps clapping their hands to rhythmic beats were sometimes surprised by a Seeger sing-along. "The concert was like none I've ever seen," remarked one writer in the Rhode Island *Providence Journal*. "He let us sing the ballads with him."[21]

When at home Seeger taught at the Downtown Community School in Greenwich Village and sang at Camp Woodland in the nearby Catskill Mountains. Wherever he was he delighted in intro-

Pete teaching people to play the banjo at a summer camp (Collection of Pete and Toshi Seeger)

ducing old songs he had learned from his work with Alan Lomax or songs from abroad. And he continued writing.

Songs came to Seeger at odd times. In 1955, as he sat in a plane heading for a concert at Oberlin College in Ohio, he found in his pocket several lines he copied from *And Quiet Flows the Don,* a novel by the Soviet author Mikhail Sholokhov. The lines described Cossack soldiers singing as they went off to serve in the tsar's army. They came from a Ukrainian folk song:

> Where are the flowers? The girls have plucked them.
> Where are the girls? They've taken husbands.
> Where are the men? They're all in the army.

Now he remembered a four-syllable musical phrase he had been carrying around in his head: "long time passing." Putting the different parts together, he came up with: "Where have all the flowers gone—long time passing." A melody from an Irish American lumberjack song carried him one step further, and finally he added what he later called "the handwringer's perennial complaint": "When will they ever learn?" In twenty minutes he had a new song. That evening, he taped the words to a microphone and sang them for the first time.

The song was simple, lyrical, and repetitive. As the United States found itself confronting the Soviet Union and Seeger faced a confrontation of his own with anti-Communists, the song had an unmistakable political message. It began simply:

> Where have all the flowers gone?
> Long time passing
> Where have all the flowers gone?
> Long time ago—

> Where have all the flowers gone?
> Girls have picked them ev'ry one
> Oh, when will you ever learn?
> Oh, when will you ever learn?

As Seeger originally wrote it, the song had but two more verses:

> Where have all the young girls gone?
> Long time passing
> Where have all the young girls gone?
> Long time ago—
> Where have all the young girls gone?
> They've taken husbands every one.
> When will they ever learn?
> When will they ever learn?
>
> Where have all the young men gone?
> Long time passing
> Where have all the young men gone?
> Long time ago—
> Where have all the young men gone?
> They're all in uniform.
> Oh, when will *we* ever learn?
> Oh, when will *we* ever learn?[22]

The song was an intensely personal plea to help create a more peaceful world. It conveyed a sense of sadness at the military struggles that killed the young, and it was particularly poignant at the height of the Cold War, when quiet conflict threatened to erupt into devastating war. It reflected the values that had guided Seeger all his life and underscored the need for accommodation rather than armed clash.

Seeger recorded the song on the Folkways label. Moses Asch, a folk music fan who owned Folkways and ran it on a shoestring, always had time for Seeger and provided him with the chance to make his music available. But within months Seeger stopped singing it, thinking it was a flop.

Others had a different opinion. Joe Hickerson, head of the Oberlin College Folksong Club, continued singing it and contributed a couple of his own verses. The next summer, when Hickerson was the music counselor at Camp Woodland, he added rhythm to the song and tried out different verses on the campers. Peter Yarrow, Noel Paul Stookey, and Mary Travers were just beginning to sing together as Peter, Paul and Mary in Greenwich Village, and they, too, picked up the song. The Kingston Trio, a major force in the folk music revival of the late 1950s and early 1960s, recorded the song without knowing it was Seeger's. Friendly with the group, as he was with virtually every folksinger in the country, Seeger told the Trio he had written it. "Oh, Pete, we didn't know," confessed Dave Guard, a member of the group. "We thought it was an old song. We'll take our name off of it." Pete's younger half-sister, Peggy, a folksinger herself, echoed the enthusiasm of other singers, telling him it was his best song. Singer and actress Marlene Dietrich, likely agreeing, sang a German translation around the world.[23]

Seeger was carving out a new career, but once again politics threatened to derail it. Intent on uncovering subversive influence wherever committee members thought it existed, HUAC had been investigating singers. The popular folksingers Josh White and Burl Ives were called into hearings. Both testified, and their compliance troubled Seeger, who felt that the committee had no business examining personal beliefs. Now, in August 1955, it was his turn.

While he was building a barn on his property in Beacon, a black car wound its way up the driveway. A stranger in a suit got out and asked, "Are you Pete Seeger?" Seeger said yes. "I've got something for you," the man said, and handed him an envelope from the U.S. government. It was a subpoena, a legal document demanding his appearance in a hearing before HUAC.[24]

Seeger had only a few weeks to decide what to do. Toshi, always organized, hired Paul Ross, a Madison Avenue lawyer who had once worked closely with the colorful New York mayor Fiorello La Guardia. Ross represented both Pete and Lee Hays, who was scheduled to appear before the same panel.

More important than finding counsel was deciding how to respond to the committee. Pete watched as some witnesses did what HUAC demanded, naming names of people with whom they worked on radical causes and describing their own activities and those of others. Such capitulation struck him as spineless. Others invoked the Fifth Amendment to the Constitution, which provides protection against self-incrimination. Although doing so lay within the boundaries of legality, the invocation could convey the impression that such witnesses had something to hide. In an atmosphere of fear and political anxiety, that implication could compromise a career. Still others confronted the committee on the basis of the First Amendment, which guaranteed the right to free speech. These witnesses argued that they had the right to say whatever they wished without being challenged by the committee or required to explain themselves. But that strategy might well entail a long and costly legal battle to achieve a dubious victory, for the committee could hold these witnesses in contempt. And witnesses who had taken that tack had not always been successful.

Ten Hollywood writers and directors had challenged the committee in 1947 and gone to jail for contempt of Congress.

Lee Hays appeared before HUAC first in what proved to be an intimidating encounter for him. As he entered the hearing room on August 16, he passed two hefty federal marshals. One said to the other, "I'd like to take them all out in the courtyard and shoot them."[25] The interrogation began by focusing on People's Songs and its radical activities. "To questions like this," Hays said, "I am going to assert my privilege under the fifth amendment because I do not believe that the purpose of this inquiry allows anyone a right to examine into my associations and my beliefs and my personal private convictions." When later asked, "Were you a member of the Communist Party on January 11, 1938?" he again invoked the Fifth Amendment. "Were you a member of the Communist Party from 1949 until the time your association with the Weavers terminated?" The same response. "Are you a member of the Communist Party now?" The reply: "I decline to answer for the same reasons."[26] Though he weathered the ordeal, he paid a price: "I don't think I have ever felt so damned alone as on that day." Even worse was the physical strain: "When I got home my heart hurt and I place the beginnings of my heart trouble at that day."[27]

Seeger came next. He was defiant from the start. "I was peculiarly able to do it," he observed. "After all, there was no job I could be fired from."[28] He told his attorney about his plan: "I want to get up there and attack these guys for what they are, the worst of America." Paul Ross counseled him to keep cool: "Don't try and be a smartass. Don't be clever. Be polite and answer the question; if you're not going to answer it, say why."[29]

Pete at HUAC hearing (© Bettmann/CORBIS)

As his interrogation began, Seeger answered the first few questions. Asked for his profession or occupation, he could not keep from sounding snide: "Well, I have worked at many things, and my main profession is a student of American folklore, and I make my living as a banjo picker, sort of damning in some people's opinions." As the committee sharpened its focus on possible Communist Party activities, Seeger replied, "I am not going to answer any questions as to my associations, my philosophical or religious beliefs or my political beliefs, or how I voted in any election or any of these private affairs. I think these are very improper questions for any American to be asked, especially under such compulsion as this."

Asked about *Daily Worker* articles and advertisements showing him singing at various affairs, Seeger's irritation grew palpable. "I feel that in my whole life I have never done anything of any conspiratorial nature," he told Chairman Francis Walter, "and I resent very much and very deeply the implication of being called before this committee that in some way because my opinions may be different from yours,...that I am any less of an American than anybody else. I love my country very deeply, sir."[30]

Puzzled by some of these responses, one committee member wanted to make sure that the singer was not invoking the Fifth Amendment. Seeger acknowledged as much, while making clear that he was not deprecating those witnesses who had.

The committee turned to the matter of Seeger's songs. Chairman Walter and Chief Counsel Frank Tavenner asked if the folksinger had sung "Wasn't That a Time." Coauthored by Lee Hays, the song began with a description of the terrible conditions American soldiers faced at Valley Forge and Gettysburg, followed by a verse about the perils of fascism and another that was indirectly—and unmistakably—critical of the current inquisition:

> And once again the madmen came,
> And should our victory fail?
> There is no vict'ry in a land
> When free men go to jail.[31]

To "Did you sing that song?" Seeger replied, "I can sing it,... [but] I don't know how well I can do it without my banjo." The committee rejected his offer. Pressed to divulge whether he had performed before Communist audiences, he retorted, "I have sung for Americans of every political persuasion, and I am proud that I never refuse to sing for an audience, no matter what religion or color of their skin, or situation of life. I have sung in hobo jungles, and I have sung for the Rockefellers, and I am proud that I have never refused to sing for anybody."[32]

Seeger made his point. He won the verbal battle. But as he looked back on his appearance before the committee, he regretted that he had not been more aggressive. A year earlier, fellow singer and friend Paul Robeson had treated his hearing with furious disdain, calling parts of the process "nonsense," but Seeger remained calm.[33] It didn't matter. He failed to answer the questions asked and instead insisted on his right to free speech. Neither course pleased the committee members. Now Seeger faced possible charges of contempt of Congress.

HUAC took its time. Finally, on July 25, 1956, a full year after the hearing, the U.S. House of Representatives cited Seeger and several others for contempt. Nine months later, on March 26, 1957, a federal grand jury indicted him on ten counts of contempt of Congress. Three days after that he pleaded not guilty to all charges and was released on bail.

Despite the specter of a looming court fight, Seeger was confident that he was doing the right thing. "I still feel I committed no wrong, and that my children will not feel ashamed of me in future years," he said to friends. "If only we could look down like the Gods upon the scene, it might even appear funny, if it were not also tragic."[34]

The indictment came as no surprise but caused Pete more trouble than he expected. The judge required him to obtain permission any time he left the Southern District of New York, a nuisance for a singer with bookings all over the country. Eventually his attorney managed to have the court accept simple notification of travel. But even notification proved an annoyance. Adverse

publicity from the HUAC hearings and the subsequent indictment led to some cancellations, though Pete remained optimistic: "Being indicted just gave me a lot of free publicity."[35]

From every corner of the country people responded to Toshi's
mailings about Pete's availability, and Seeger found himself away
from home much of the time. While he basked in the glow of
appreciative audiences, "Toshi had it hard," he recalled. "[She]
had to face people in Beacon week after week all during this, and
I was just off traveling, getting applause everywhere I appeared.
She didn't get any applause; she just had to take the snubs of some
of the people in town."[36]

Meanwhile, Paul Ross was handling the legal issues. He recognized that simply calling HUAC's questions "immoral" or
"improper" wouldn't stand a chance in court. He understood
that the best hope for acquittal was to raise technical questions
about the indictment. Federal courts in the late 1950s had begun
to overturn convictions of uncooperative witnesses when they
deemed indictments faulty. Ross chose that approach.

After the indictment Seeger assumed his case would come to
trial quickly. He was mistaken. The government took its time;
months turned into years. Minor victories spawned hope for
Seeger. When Ross sought to subpoena the HUAC chairman to
testify in the forthcoming trial, the government filed a motion to
quash the subpoena on the grounds that "compliance therewith
would be unreasonable and oppressive." The U.S. District Court
refused to so rule in advance.[37]

With his trial about to begin in 1961, Seeger held his own version of a news conference at the Park-Sheraton Hotel in New York
City. On his lawyer's advice he declined to comment about the

trial itself, but he did speak about three songs HUAC had mentioned. These were songs, he said, that he had offered to sing at the hearing, but the committee was not interested. Now he took the opportunity to sing them before an audience of journalists. First he sang an a cappella version of "The Hammer Song." The rhythms were contagious and the newsmen were soon tapping their toes. Next came "Wasn't That a Time," with Pete accompanying himself on the banjo. The last selection was a song by Lead Belly, the former black convict who had long suffered his own kind of discrimination. As Seeger sang "Midnight Special," the newsmen broke into applause. He would sing for anyone, he said: "I'm proud I can bring good songs to the people. I'm a catalyst cutting across lines." He read a statement that Carl Sandburg had phoned to him. "I would put Pete Seeger in the first rank of American folk singers," the poet observed. "I think he ought to be a free man, roving the American landscape, singing for the audiences who love him, Republican, Democrat, and independents."[38]

On March 27, 1961, the trial began. Five hundred spectators packed the courtroom. Judge Thomas Murphy, formerly a district attorney who had once heard the Weavers sing at the Blue Angel club in New York, presided, with a jury of eight men and four women. Irving Younger, assistant U.S. attorney, opened by stressing that this was a case not about Seeger's Communist Party membership but solely about whether he was guilty of criminal contempt: "Did this defendant commit the crime which I call the contempt of Congress on the date in question as charged in the indictment? That is all there is to it." Paul Ross, in turn, told the jury that no government body had the right to ask the questions HUAC had asked Seeger. "Now it is our contention," he said, "that in this case, and in this investigation of the entertainment industry there was no question of the national security involved, there was no question of any action to overthrow the government by force and violence, not at all, and there were no questions at any time to any of the witnesses in that investigation, including Peter Seeger, which dealt with that particular subject, or any subject relevant to it."[39]

In the course of the trial, Ross called Congressman Walter to the stand in an effort to establish that HUAC served no legitimate legislative purpose in its hearings. Rather, it was simply seeking to expose and identify Communists or former Communists in the entertainment industry, to drive them from their jobs and prevent them from securing employment. Walter denied that characterization of HUAC's purpose. In attempting to challenge Walter, Ross's line of questioning hit roadblock after roadblock as Attorney Younger objected. Judge Murphy upheld most of the objections, excluding more than one hundred questions, and ordered the jury to leave the courtroom during the challenge to HUAC's authority.[40] Seeger, never called to testify, was in trouble. As one reporter observed, "Seeger will be lucky if he gets off with the electric chair at this rate."[41]

Judge Murphy's charge to the jury only confirmed what was obvious during testimony. HUAC's questions, he told the members, were legal and legitimate and were connected to the committee's investigations. The jury deliberated for an hour and twenty minutes and returned with guilty verdicts on all ten counts of contempt.

Six days later the folksinger reappeared in court for sentencing. Before handing down the sentence, Murphy asked Seeger whether he was a Communist. Seeger again refused to answer and instead offered a short statement of his own. "After having heard myself talked about pro and con for three days," he said, "I am grateful for the chance to say a few words, unrestricted words myself." He insisted, "I have never in my life said or supported or done anything in any way subversive to my country." He noted, "The House committee wanted to pillory me because it didn't like some few of the many thousands of places I have sung. Now, it so happens that the specific song whose title was mentioned in this trial ['Wasn't That a Time'] was not permitted to be sung at the time. It is one of my favorites. The song is apropos to this trial, and I wondered if I might have your permission to sing it here before I close?"

"You may not," the judge responded.

Unperturbed, Seeger went on: "Well, perhaps you will hear it some other time. A good song can only do good, and I am proud of the songs I have sung. I hope to be able to continue to sing them for all who want to listen, Republicans, Democrats, or Independents, for as long as I live."[42]

Judge Murphy sentenced Seeger to a year in prison for each of the ten counts of contempt, to be served concurrently, so that Seeger would be free in a year. At the same time the judge denied Seeger bail and told the bailiff to take the defendant away. Seeger's attorney convinced the court of appeals to permit bail, and friends raised the $2,000 to secure his release after several hours in jail while he appealed the conviction.

In the spring of 1962, the U.S. Court of Appeals finally heard the case. Judge Irving Kaufman, who had presided over the trial that sent Julius and Ethel Rosenberg to the electric chair for passing atomic secrets to the Russians, oversaw the proceedings. After hearing arguments, he overturned Seeger's conviction on a technicality. "The indictment," he declared, "was defective because it failed to properly allege the authority of the subcommittee to conduct the hearings in issue, and to set forth the basis of that authority accurately."[43] The government chose not to seek another indictment. Seeger was free.

Pete was elated. After years of living under a legal cloud he could finally move on. Friends helped him celebrate and sympathetic newspapers hailed the verdict. The decision was "a return to reason," according to the *New York Post*.[44] Although the victory was won on a technicality, it was still a victory over an abrasive, abusive committee that had far exceeded its authority, Seeger believed, and he felt vindicated. His faith in America, however naïve at times, remained unshaken. "I really believed," he said, "and I think I was right, that in the long run, this country doesn't go in for things like that."[45]

Now he could continue undistracted on his self-appointed task of using music to protest injustice in America, as he had all his life. Unbowed, he joined rallies and demonstrations against the nuclear testing that he knew was poisoning the earth's atmosphere and threatening the survival of the human race.

At the same time he made a professional shift. Just before Pete's case went to trial, the jazz expert John Hammond asked Seeger to record with Columbia Records. His old friend Moses Asch agreed that recording with Columbia would provide him access to an audience far larger than any he had before.

Seeger's work in summer camps and colleges had paid off for him and for many others. He became a master musician, able to captivate an audience and get people singing along with him. A whole generation of youngsters learned his songs. A new wave of folksingers—the Kingston Trio, Joan Baez, Peter, Paul and Mary, Bob Dylan, Tom Paxton, Phil Ochs, and others—came onto the

Pete protesting the manufacture and testing of bombs (Collection of Pete and Toshi Seeger)

scene, men and women whose path he lit and who looked up to him. He was only too happy to work with them and relished their singing his songs as he learned theirs. "If I Had a Hammer" became hugely popular with the release of Peter, Paul and Mary's version. And the week he was acquitted, "Where Have All the Flowers Gone?" his lovely, lyrical plea for a peaceful, nonviolent world of human harmony, reached the top forty on the charts. *Time* magazine called him "the current patriarch of folksinging."[46] At long last, Seeger felt, people were listening to his music and he was making a difference. His success in getting others to sing—something he had sought all his life—was a testament to the power of song.

· *Four* ·

"WE SHALL OVERCOME"

∾

W ITH HIS LEGAL TROUBLES BEHIND HIM, SEEGER FELT HOPEFUL about the future. The victory in the appeal of his contempt conviction signaled that the worst excesses of the Red Scare might be over. And there were other promising signs of change. The placid political mood of the 1950s, personified by the avuncular President Dwight D. Eisenhower, was giving way to a new exuberance and activism, characterized by the youthful, photogenic John F. Kennedy, Seeger's classmate at Harvard and now president of the United States. Reflecting the growing optimism, students, mostly black but also white, were joining the African American struggle for civil rights. Reform—real reform of the kind Seeger had been pursuing for a quarter of a century—might be possible at last.

Seeger still faced obstacles in his own path. Some people continued to see him as a radical, and they frequently had a say in what opportunities came his way. In early 1963 CBS-TV asked Seeger and the Weavers to be part of a program called *Dinner with the President,* sponsored by the Anti-Defamation League of the Jewish organization B'nai B'rith. Seeger was delighted. He had long hoped to popularize American music through television and was eager to perform. But then Anti-Defamation League officials invoked the blacklist of the 1950s and made the appearance impossible.

At about the same time ABC-TV was embarking on a weekly folk music series called *Hootenanny*. What better, or bigger, audience for his music than viewers who watched every week? Seeger wanted to be part of it. One of the consultants helping to plan the program assured the singer that he would be included, but after the network filmed the first few shows Seeger had yet to sing on screen. An associate producer explained that neither Pete nor the Weavers would ever appear on the show because of "pressure from advertising agencies, sponsors, and stations."[1] Once again others' fear co-opted Seeger. Despite his growing popularity and his vindication in the courts, he found himself barred from the very outlets that could bring his music to the greatest number of Americans.

Rumors, most as vicious as they were false, circulated about what had happened. A story in the *San Francisco Chronicle* claimed that the singer was "too slow and thoughtful" for the TV show.[2] At a press conference a few months later, *Hootenanny*'s executive producer, Richard Lewine, underscored the idea that the increasingly well-known folksinger was a lackluster performer with the comment, "Pete Seeger just can't hold an audience."[3]

A few network officials came clean. They blamed sponsor Procter & Gamble, maker of Tide detergent and other household products, for rejecting a radical figure whose very name might cost them sales. "I actually get hot and flushed just thinking about it," Seeger said. "We have all this richness and variety in our country but a bunch of schmoes, out to sell soap, keep the whole country seeing the same dreary things night after night."[4] Some folk music fans called for a boycott of the program, and some singers refused to perform on it. But the show—without Seeger—went on.

Hootenanny marked an important point in the history of American folk music. Its popularity was reaching a new peak, in part because Seeger himself had helped to create an audience for the music, both old songs and many of his own new ones. The fact of its success was the irony of Seeger's career. As millions of youngsters embraced the music he sang, sponsors rejected him.

Those youngsters were part of the huge boom of babies born at the end of World War II or in the immediate postwar years. They were growing up, questioning the values, as well as the musical tastes, of their parents. They responded eagerly to what they regarded as the new folk music beginning to appear everywhere, even on television. Folk music, of course, was hardly new, and it came from everywhere, as Pete understood better than most. "Some of the best music in our country is made by unlettered farmers, miners, housewives," he once explained.[5]

His life had paralleled the rising interest in old folk tunes. As he came of age musically, some classical singers in the 1930s, including the contralto Marion Anderson and the baritone Paul Robeson, brought folk music into the concert hall. Throughout the 1940s and 1950s, Seeger helped to stimulate what became a folk revival. "Go back to that night…when Pete first met Woody Guthrie," Alan Lomax observed. "You can date the renascence of American folk song from that night."[6]

Seeger hoped to create such a broad singing movement with the union songs in the 1930s. He failed, however, to mobilize mass

Pete performing in the 1950s (Collection of Pete and Toshi Seeger)

support for labor causes. Now he became the influential figure he had always hoped to be as the folk music he loved skyrocketed in popularity. His talent and energy fed the folk boom, despite his being barred from television and other commercial venues.

Public interest soared when the Kingston Trio recorded the song "Tom Dooley" in 1958. Four years earlier, after a concert at the Palo Alto High School gym in California, Seeger, the featured performer, had sold a copy of his booklet *How to Play the 5-String Banjo* to Dave Guard, a Stanford University sophomore. Guard and two friends, Nick Reynolds and Bob Shane, followed the Weavers' footsteps by forming a group of their own. They called themselves the Kingston Trio in an effort to capitalize on the Jamaican calypso sound of the popular Harry Belafonte.

Auditioning for a job at the Purple Onion, a San Francisco nightclub, the group heard a song about a murder by Civil War veteran Tom Dula in 1866. Sung widely in North Carolina and Tennessee, it became popular in the 1940s, and Alan Lomax printed a version of it in 1947 in *Folk Song U.S.A.* Haunted by the melody, the trio found words in another collection, recorded the song as "Tom Dooley," and rode its popularity to a number one hit.

Other young singers were also following Seeger's lead. At that same high school concert in Palo Alto, thirteen-year-old Joan and nine-year-old Mimi Baez heard Seeger for the first time. Daughters of a California physicist and his wife, the girls came to the concert with their aunt Tia, who liked Seeger. She thought, "If I still had some influence on those girls, they should hear something they weren't going to hear on the radio."[7] As he performed, Seeger followed his standard pattern, what he called "a cultural guerrilla tactic": "I sang songs about people from all walks of life, and I talked about how anyone from any walk of life could sing this kind of song himself." Looking out over his audience he would say, "Sing with me. Sing by yourself. Make your own music. Pick up a guitar, or just sing a cappella. We don't need professional singers. We don't need stars. You can sing. Join me now."[8]

The message struck a resonant chord with the two girls. After the concert young Joan Baez looked in the mirror, recalled Seeger's advice, and said to herself, "I can be a singer, too."[9] When her father took a job at the Massachusetts Institute of Technology in early 1958, the family moved to a house near Boston and Joan enrolled at Boston University. In no time she was singing at the Café Yana, the Club 47, and other coffeehouses in Harvard Square.

Still another group, Peter, Paul and Mary, built a folk music following that crossed borders. Under the guidance of manager Albert Grossman, Peter Yarrow and Noel Paul Stookey teamed up with Mary Travers, an apple-cheeked blonde with a deep, rich voice. The new group sang in harmonies that reminded listeners of the Weavers.[10] Singing a number of Seeger's songs, they gave the Weavers greater national and even international attention.

Bob Dylan, originally Bob Zimmerman from Minnesota, became the near-child prodigy of the folk music movement. Arriving in New York he performed, recorded, and wrote his own music. His lyrics were poetic, his melodies languid and wailing. When he sang his voice was nasal and rasping. On college campuses across the nation his songs soon became the anthems of a generation. Greenwich Village folksingers recognized his enormous talent and encouraged him. To Dylan, Pete Seeger was "a living saint."[11]

To support the growing interest in folk music, Toshi Seeger helped to create what became the Newport Folk Festival. She had long played a role in organizing Pete's career. Now she turned her skills to the movement he was nurturing. The increasing popularity of the genre captured the attention of commercial advertisers, agencies, and record companies, who attempted to take control of the music. But Toshi, with the aid of Pete's manager,

Harold Leventhal, dreamed of a festival where performers made the musical decisions and received equal pay.

Newport, Rhode Island, a place containing summer homes for many of the wealthy industrialists and financiers of the late nineteenth century, had hosted a jazz festival since 1954. In 1959, as folk music caught on, the Seegers and other organizers proposed an afternoon of folksinging to follow the jazz festival. That year the Kingston Trio performed, as did the bluegrass banjo player Earl Scruggs and Bob Gibson, another folksinger whose career Seeger encouraged. Gibson brought Joan Baez with him to sing on stage, gaining for her valuable public exposure that helped her career take off.[12] Rioting by boisterous fans ended the 1960 jazz festival, but in 1963 the Newport Folk Foundation revived the folk festival. Pete and his half-brother Mike wanted greater variety, venues for both religious and political songs, and equitable representation of old and young, new and established, and male and female performers. The festival that year, and for the next several years, captured the spirit of the folk revival.

Folk music was becoming a powerful force, though it still evoked sneers from mainstream critics. In early 1962, *Time* magazine vented its disapproval, inadvertently capturing the musical mood: "Guitar atwangle, eyes aimed into a far corner, the voice pitched in a keening wail, the singer holds the rapt attention of the shaggy boys, girls and dogs scattered around his Greenwich Village pad." College students were not the only ones buying and playing guitars for the first time. All kinds of people discovered that with a few simple chords they could sing songs and amuse their friends.[13]

In the late 1950s and early 1960s, folk music acquired a new focus. Since his days at Harvard Seeger had sought to use his music to promote peace and social justice, whether in factories or in the larger world of politics and international relations. What Eleanor Roosevelt once called a "rising wind" of freedom was blowing across the land, and folk music sounded its name.

The civil rights movement had its roots in America's troubled racial past. Discrimination, a legacy of slavery, persisted into the twentieth century. Rigid patterns of racial exclusion remained the norm in the South. The so-called Jim Crow system of segregation divided the nation in two, creating "separate but equal" public facilities in everything from schools to bathrooms to drinking fountains. But separate facilities were seldom equal. Organizations such as the National Association for the Advancement of Colored People (NAACP), founded in 1910, pressed for equal rights, and the Congress of Racial Equality, established in 1942, sought change through peaceful confrontation.

Protests against discrimination and segregation during World War II sowed the seeds for more assertive efforts in the postwar years. The bombshell *Brown v. Board of Education* ruling by the U.S. Supreme Court in 1954 mandated that "separate but equal" schools were no longer constitutional. The following year, in Montgomery, Alabama, a black seamstress, Rosa Parks, sat down in the all-white section of a public bus. When she refused to move, police arrested her for violating segregation laws. Led by twenty-seven-year-old Martin Luther King, Jr., the new pastor of the Dexter Avenue Baptist Church, the black citizens of Montgomery boycotted the bus system. For more than a year African Americans walked to work until a new city ordinance, the result of a Supreme Court ruling against segregation on Montgomery's buses, permitted them to sit wherever they wished.

Seeger watched the growing agitation with interest. He had known few black people in his school days. Only when he dropped out of Harvard and moved to New York did he learn about the patterns of segregation and the horrors of lynching. He followed civil rights issues through articles in the *New Masses* and the *Daily Worker*. Preoccupied first with the labor movement and later with anti-Communists, he "didn't foresee the civil rights movement," but he had always felt strongly about issues of justice and equality and so found himself drawn to the cause.[14]

Seeger also encountered racial prejudice closer to home. Irritated by sometimes intolerant comments by Pete's mother during a visit with her in Florida, Toshi once turned into a beach entrance marked "Colored." When an appalled Constance asked why a Japanese American would use that entrance, Toshi replied, "Well, after all, I'm colored, you know."[15] Seeger and his family were also the targets of vicious racial epithets at the Peekskill concert in 1949, when Pete sang with Paul Robeson.

In 1955, Seeger read about the Montgomery bus boycott in the *New York Times*. He was intrigued by the protest and interested to learn that the protesters were singing songs. He was determined to find out more: "I wrote...or telephoned the reporter and said, 'What's the name of the organization? What's their address?' And he gives me the address of the Montgomery Improvement Association." Pete wrote to the activists, mailing a $25 contribution along with a letter asking them, "Send me copies of some of your songs. We'd like to learn them up here."

E. D. Nixon, head of the local branch of the NAACP organizing the boycott, sent him a thank-you note that included a little mimeographed song sheet. One of the songs caught Seeger's fancy as he read the lyrics: "We are moving on to victory. We are moving on to victory. We are moving on to victory, and we know the time ain't long. We know love is the watchword. We know love is the watchword. To the tune of 'Give Me That Old Time Religion.'"[16] A year later he met Martin Luther King, Jr., in person at the Highlander Folk School. Later he flew to Birmingham to sing at a rally with King and the Montgomery Improvement Association. Another thank-you note, this one from King, acknowledged his "moral support and Christian generosity."[17]

Seeger had been intrigued with southern songs he heard on his 1936 trip with his father to the folk song and dance festival

Pete with Martin Luther King, Jr., Rosa Parks, and others at Highlander (Collection of Pete and Toshi Seeger)

in Asheville, North Carolina. The music, with its lively rhythms, fired his ambition to play the banjo, and southern songs soon became a part of his repertoire.

His interest took him to Highlander, which he knew from past visits. The school was founded in 1932 in New Market, Tennessee, by Miles and Zilphia Horton as a reflection of their dedication to social change. Its earliest commitments lay with labor organizing and the education of working men and women. As the union movement grew in the New Deal years, Highlander served as a training ground for labor organizers and activists. Seeger and Woody Guthrie stopped there in 1940 on their way to Texas, and three years later, when Pete was stationed in Alabama during the war, he made a point of using a rare weekend pass to visit.

In 1946, while working as the music director at Highlander, Zilphia Horton heard striking black tobacco workers singing to keep up their spirits. Their song was "We Will Overcome," based loosely on an old spiritual called "I'll Be All Right." Sung very slowly, it became her favorite song. Seeger learned it from her in 1947 and published it in *People's Songs* that year. He sped up the tempo, singing it with a banjo rhythm, and made a significant change.[18] "We Will Overcome" became "We Shall Overcome." Why the change? "Toshi kids me that it was my Harvard grammar," he later recalled, "but I think I liked a more open sound; 'We will' has alliteration to it, but 'We shall' opens the mouth wider; the 'i' in 'will' is not an easy vowel to sing well."[19] He also added a number of verses, as Horton had done herself.

The song reached the folksinger Frank Hamilton in 1952. He taught it to Guy Carawan, an MA student from Los Angeles spending more and more time in the South. Martin Luther King, Jr., heard Seeger sing it for a crowd in 1957. The following day, driving to another speaking engagement, King observed, "That song really sticks with you, doesn't it?"[20]

It stuck with Carawan when in 1959 he came to Highlander to work as a song leader. A year later, as African American students in Greensboro, North Carolina, and Nashville, Tennessee, launched sit-in demonstrations at lunch counters where blacks were refused service, Carawan organized a weekend for activists at Highlander called "Sing for Freedom." He invited Seeger and other musicians to help him. As they sang "We Shall Overcome," Hamilton and Carawan slowed the song down and taught it to civil rights workers that way. "It was," Seeger said, "the hit song of the weekend."[21]

Several weeks later, at another conference in Raleigh, North Carolina, that led to the founding of the Student Nonviolent Coordinating Committee (SNCC), somebody shouted, "Guy, teach us all 'We Shall Overcome.'" He did, noted Seeger, "and that's when they invented the way of crossing your hands in front of you so your left hand reaches to your right and grasps the right hand of the person to your right...and your right hand reaches to the left and grasps the left hand of somebody on your left. And your shoulders almost touch as you sway back and forth."[22] The gesture became a sign of solidarity among civil rights activists across the country. Accepting the slower tempo, Seeger and others helped spread the song. In June 1963, he recorded it at Carnegie Hall in New York. In no time people were singing it at rallies and marches nationwide.

"We Shall Overcome" became the marching song of the movement. It had a quiet simplicity that reflected the passion of activists' commitment to social justice and the strength of their resolve to bring about social change:

> We shall overcome, we shall overcome,
> We shall overcome some day.
> Deep in my heart, I do believe,
> We shall overcome some day.

Other verses, equally simple, carried the same message. One declared, "We'll walk hand in hand," while another proclaimed, "We shall live in peace."[23] Singers could add verses of their own, keeping the song going as long as they chose.

Music became an integral part of the civil rights movement. As Guy Carawan and his wife, Candie, noted later of the songs, "The important ones are the old, slow-paced spirituals and hymns that sing of hope and determination and the rhythmic jubilee spirituals and bright gospel songs that protest boldly and celebrate eventual victory."[24] The Carawans hit the right explanatory note: the power of these kinds of songs reflected the confidence that boycotts and sit-ins would succeed. As protestors marched arm in arm, their voices lifted in song and the rhythmic beat of the spiritual and gospel tunes gave them a sense of solidarity.

African American churches have always used music in worship, but such songs didn't necessarily become significant in the social protest movement. Indeed, in the early years of the civil rights struggle, music sometimes seemed to work at cross purposes with the demands for change. The Reverend C. T. Vivian, who presided over a church in Nashville in the early 1960s, recalled one occasion when he was giving a speech on behalf of the movement. The choir followed it up with the gospel song "I'll

Fly Away," which he said conveyed the wrong message altogether. It reflected an effort to escape troubled times rather than a commitment to make conditions better.

The efforts at Highlander to promote a musical movement made a difference. Carawan later acknowledged his debt to Seeger. "I had been greatly influenced by Pete," he said, "struck by his exciting way of playing the banjo and his collection of songs from grassroots America."[25] It was at Seeger's suggestion that the Carawans "came to Highlander and tried to carry on Zilphia's way of working with people" after her death. Carawan did what Seeger had always done: he changed words and adapted old songs to new purposes, he got audiences singing, and he conveyed his own dedication to the cause. No one who heard him could mistake his enthusiasm for a song or miss its deeper meaning. His approach worked. As Reverend Vivian recalled, "Guy had taken the song 'Follow the Drinking Gourd,' and I didn't know the song, but he gave some background on it and boom, that began to make sense. And little by little, spiritual after spiritual after spiritual began to appear with new sets of words, new changes. 'Keep Your Eyes on the Prize, Hold On' or 'I'm Gonna Sit at the Welcome Table.' Once we had seen it done, we could begin to do it."[26]

Singing caught on and became the basis of Seeger's growing involvement in the civil rights movement. Here was another cause to which he could contribute his musical talents. He was especially fond of the old gospel song "Oh, Mary, Don't You Weep" and performed it regularly. Introducing it on one occasion, he noted, "Some people call them spirituals, some call them gospel songs. Whatever they want to call them, they come out of the churches of the South. They have African rhythms and melodies and harmonies,...but it's all American."[27] Like so many gospel songs, it had simple lyrics, a catchy tune, and an upbeat message based on the escape of the Israelites from Egypt. In response to the injunction in the chorus, "Oh Mary, don't you weep, don't you mourn," repeated twice, came the reason for optimism: "Pharaoh's army got drownded," which led to freedom for the children of Israel. As he did so often, Seeger added verses and embellished the song. He especially liked a verse Lead Belly sang: "Moses stood on the Red Sea shore. Smotin' the water with a two-by-four." He was also taken with what he called "that absolutely world shaking verse: 'God gave Noah the rainbow sign. No more water but the fire next time.'"[28] The message was clear: God would do whatever was necessary to help the cause of freedom.

Seeger used the song to galvanize audiences by asking them to join him. As he strummed his banjo, he first sang several verses, then he stopped singing, continued strumming, and challenged the crowd: "We got to sing this even better than this. We got to sing it so they hear it down in Washington, D.C., in London, Moscow, Peking, Tokyo, everywhere else."[29] Audiences couldn't resist and did as he asked.

With his energy, enthusiasm, and overwhelming sense of commitment, Seeger sang wherever he could in support of the civil rights movement. In February 1961, he performed, along with Carawan and others, in a benefit concert at Carnegie Hall to help Highlander. The musicians included two southern groups, the female Montgomery Gospel Trio and the male Nashville Quartet. As Freedom Rides began that year, with black and white volunteers riding together on interstate buses to integrate segregated southern bus terminals, he sang to support that cause. He and others raised money for UCLA Freedom Riders at a concert in Santa Monica. In 1962 he used many of his concert dates to press for civil rights with songs like "We Shall Overcome" that created a sense of confidence that the cause of equality would triumph in the end. In the spring of that year he performed in Newark, New Jersey, a week later in Chicago, a few days after that in Winnipeg in Canada, then on to Washington, D.C., and New York. With his round-the-clock activity he exhausted himself. At one point the folksinger Judy Collins found him after a meeting asleep on the floor of a house in New York, too tired to drive home. Toshi was worried and finally told him, "Look, you have to ease up—you're going to drop dead if you don't."[30]

Pete with Bernice Reagon in the 1960s (Collection of Pete and Toshi Seeger)

Always a mentor and a model, he befriended younger singers and encouraged them both in music and in the movement.
In the fall of 1962 he met nineteen-year-old Bernice Johnson, a
student at Spelman College with a resonant voice and a growing
reputation as a civil rights singer. Seeger pushed her to start a
group of SNCC singers who could help create a following for civil
rights. She dropped out of school, phoned Toshi, and asked her to
organize a tour for the new ensemble, the Freedom Singers. Pete
made sure the group sang at Newport in 1963 and 1964. He also
took Bob Dylan on his first venture to the South, where he sang
his own song "Blowin' in the Wind." It became a huge popular

Pete with the Freedom Singers (Collection of Pete and Toshi Seeger)

hit, rising to the top of the pop music charts, particularly in the version sung by Peter, Paul and Mary.[31]

In the fall of 1962, Seeger learned a memorable lesson about the great racial divide separating blacks and even well-meaning whites. King and his movement, the Southern Christian Leadership Conference (SCLC), decided to make a major assault on segregation in Albany, Georgia, a small southern town with a large black population. Building on groundwork already laid by SNCC and the NAACP, King appeared at a rally in person to focus attention on the struggle. He was arrested for parading without a permit, along with hundreds of other black demonstrators.

African Americans in Albany were already using hymns in the struggle but hoped to learn something new by inviting Seeger to perform at a local black church. Seeger relished the idea of serving on the front lines of the crusade, even in hostile territory like Albany. He knew that here, as elsewhere, the White Citizens' Council was on the lookout for outside agitators who sought to overturn time-honored southern customs. Whatever the danger, Albany was where Seeger wanted to be.

The church was packed. As Seeger waited to perform the congregation sang a number of traditional hymns, adding new words more appropriate to the struggle for equal rights. Then the pastor introduced him and Pete moved to the pulpit. He had a magical knack for reading an audience, but this time the magic failed. As he started to pick a tune on his banjo, he never imagined that the instrument could be a reminder of minstrel days, when whites in blackface mimicked African American performers on stage. His usual repertoire of labor songs drew stony silence. When he tried to buy time with a long ballad, one congregant whispered to another, "If this is white folks' music, I don't think much of it." "Shush," came the response. "If we expect white folks to understand us, we've got to try to understand them."[32]

In an act of near desperation, Seeger fell back on what had already become a standard of racial resistance, "We Shall Overcome." The entire congregation joined in, for it meant something to virtually everyone there. More than labor songs or long ballads, it touched the souls of black folk facing the rancor of whites across the South. As he finished singing and left the church to polite thanks, Seeger realized that when it came to the music of race he could be tone deaf.

While throwing himself fully into the civil rights movement, Seeger continued to seek ways of appearing on television. Success was still elusive. He and Toshi decided it was time for a break. They made plans to leave the country for a year, to travel with their children around the world, singing old songs, learning new ones, and filming their adventures. Toshi made the arrangements, while manager Leventhal helped organize some foreign television appearances.

Going abroad created huge logistical problems: how to keep a family of five on track and intact, how to get to where they wanted to go, how to carry baggage and instruments to the places where Pete was to perform. But first Pete insisted on a farewell concert at Carnegie Hall. He wanted one last opportunity to sing the freedom songs of the movement to an American audience. "If you want to get out of a pessimistic mood yourself, I've got one *sure* remedy," he told a packed house as the concert began. "Go help those people in Birmingham or Mississippi."[33] Perhaps he was talking to himself as much as his fans. He launched into

"Oh, Freedom," sang a variety of other songs, and concluded with what was rapidly becoming his signature: "We Shall Overcome." The live recording, released under the title of the final song, was as successful as the concert.

Sorry to be leaving in the midst of the civil rights struggle, Seeger fixed on the idea of showing that American songs could reach people on four continents. He had faith in his music, and in its power to promote change, not just in the United States but around the globe: "[I needed] to test myself by the toughest means possible that my chosen work has a basic, universal validity." It was, he said, a "moment of truth."[34]

Before leaving, Seeger performed at the Newport Folk Festival but was gone by the time of the legendary March on Washington, where Martin Luther King, Jr., proclaimed to hundreds of thousands of demonstrators, "I have a dream." The family departed in August 1963. After visits to Samoa, Australia, and Indonesia the Seegers arrived in Japan, the birthplace of Toshi's father. Few Japanese spoke English, and sometimes audiences had trouble understanding Seeger's lyrics. So he played instrumentals and simple songs with repeated refrains, like "Where Have All the Flowers Gone?" They worked best of all.

In Calcutta, India, twenty thousand people showed up to hear him. There he performed in the presence of the American ambassador, according to the *New Delhi Statesman,* with "a fervor that is almost evangelical."[35] A nationwide radio broadcast had an audience estimated to be as large as the entire American population.

Africa proved perhaps the most challenging—and the most exciting—venue. Logistics and the bright equatorial sun complicated the Seegers' stay in Kenya, though the children and their parents delighted in driving through the country toward Tanzania. As they crossed the dusty African plain wondrous animals—zebras, elephants, and giraffes—ran beside their car. Sometimes, though, the family seemed restless, worn with the travel and tired of being cooped up with one another for days at a time. "As soon as we possibly could, we'd get away from one another to different sides of the plane or hotel room," Toshi remembered.[36]

The experience of performing abroad brought Pete to life. At a graduation ceremony in Dar es Salaam, the capital of Tanzania, he sang in a ballroom without a microphone. He could feel the strain in his voice and knew he would pay with a case of laryngitis. It was worth the price when "We Shall Overcome" set the audience ablaze with delight: "[I always know] when that marvelous moment comes—the 'click' of singer and listener—when I have really found my audience and it has really found me."[37]

As the year wore on, Seeger longed more and more for home. He heard about the upcoming Mississippi Summer Freedom Project, coordinated by SNCC, to send volunteers to that rigidly segregated state. There students and others could help register voters and establish "freedom schools" to teach black children reading and writing skills often lacking in their education. That was the kind of activism Seeger sought and he was eager to be involved. But the tantalizing prospect of joining this effort had first to await the end of the tour. The family went to Nigeria and Ghana, stopped in Europe, East and West, and finally returned to the United States in mid-1964. The ten-month journey had included stops in more than twenty-five countries.

Two months later, Seeger was in Mississippi. He arrived just as reports were circulating about three SNCC volunteers—Michael Schwerner, Andrew Goodman, and James Chaney—missing and presumably dead. Seeger, too, encountered trouble. In the terminal, after he left the plane that brought him south, a white Mississippian who had been onboard approached him. "He accosted me with blood in his eye," Seeger said.

"Are you coming down here to sing for the niggers?" the man asked with unvarnished disdain.

"I've been asked down here by some friends to sing," Seeger answered calmly. "I hope that *anyone* who wants to hear me can come."

"Well, you just better watch your step. If we weren't here now, I would knock the shit out of you."[38]

In Mississippi Seeger had a chance to do what he did best: use music to help arouse people and make peace. In Hattiesburg in August, in the words of a schoolteacher he had met years before, "Pete arrived with his guitar over his shoulder, playing."[39] In the midst of tension between black and white volunteers over who had authority, with the real threat of racial violence always present, his music helped bring a sense of calm and common cause. People singing together were less likely to struggle with one another, more willing to work together. Songs like "We Shall Overcome" helped remind them of why they had come to the South.

In the midst of a performance in Meridian that same month, a message brought the sad news everyone feared. Schwerner, Chaney, and Goodman were dead, their bodies encased in a dam. As he did so well, Seeger turned to a song to help ease the pain. Quietly, softly, he sang:

O healing river
Send down your water
Send down your water
Upon this land

O healing river
Send down your water
And wash the blood
From off our sand.[40]

He closed the concert, which had suddenly taken on the feel of a funeral, by telling the grieving audience, "We must sing 'We Shall Overcome' now. The three boys would not have wanted us to weep, but to sing and understand this song.'"[41] More than ever there was the hope that music might help bring about racial change, might provide a social cement, even in the midst of horrific violence.

Pete and Toshi returned to the South in March 1965. King and the SCLC were determined to validate the right of African Americans to vote. Despite the clear provisions of the Fifteenth Amendment guaranteeing universal suffrage, "Selma has succeeded in limiting Negro registration to the snail's pace of about 145 persons a year," King wrote in the New York Times. "At this rate, it would take 103 years to register the 15,000 eligible Negro voters of Dallas County."[42]

In protest, King led marchers to the Selma courthouse. Police descended on the crowd, dragging off protesters and arresting more than two thousand people. Another huge demonstration led to King's own arrest, along with that of 770 other protesters, many of them children. More arrests followed. In response King decided on a mass march to Montgomery, the state capital, to present grievances to the governor. As the demonstrators approached a bridge leading out of Selma, the sheriff and his men turned the demonstrators back. Troopers with bullwhips, electric cattle prods, and rubber tubes wrapped in barbed wire attacked the marchers, their actions recorded for the nation on television cameras. Viewers were horrified at the brutality, but King knew that he could not stop there. He quickly decided to organize another march. This was the one the Seegers joined.

Although armed national guardsmen were everywhere, Alabama remained a dangerous place. The comedian Dick Gregory, singers Harry Belafonte and Tony Bennett, and the actor Anthony Perkins, among other celebrities, came to march on Montgomery. Organizers were afraid of what might happen to them and other outsiders. Only hours after the Seegers crossed a road just outside of the city, Ku Klux Klan members fired on a car driven by Viola Liuzzo, a middle-aged white volunteer from Detroit, in the same spot and shot her through the head.

Singing at roadside camps at night, protesters nonetheless remained hopeful. Seeger wandered from one group to another, listening to new songs, learning different verses to old hymns. At one point, resting on the grass along Alabama's Route 80, he began writing down melodies he was hearing. A woman watching him told him, "Don't you know you can't write down freedom songs?" When he persisted in trying to get words down, people kept telling him, "Man, there are no words, you just make them up." Still he persevered, asking for a few verses that he could take home and teach to other people.[43] For him, music was at the very center of the crusade. Without "all those songs," he believed, "the civil rights movement would not have succeeded."[44]

The Montgomery march ended on a triumphant note, as the demonstrators entered the capital. But the movement was changing. The peaceful, nonviolent approach of Martin Luther King, Jr., gave way to angry calls for Black Power from SNCC's leader Stokely Carmichael and others. The gentle strains of "We Shall Overcome" faded. Seeger and his music suddenly seemed less important, out of favor. One phase of the civil rights movement, with King and his colleagues locking arms and marching in peaceful protest, was running out of steam, and Seeger was not sure what role, if any, he might play in the new, more militant phase that was emerging.

· *Five* ·

"Waist Deep in the Big Muddy"

∞

Seeger had little sense of what lay ahead when he went to the Newport Folk Festival in the summer of 1965. He opened a concert that featured many of the most popular artists in the country, including Bob Dylan. Pete was fond of the raspy-voiced singer who had already made a huge splash in the past few years. His protest songs—"Blowin' in the Wind," "Masters of War," "The Times They Are A-Changin'"—echoed around the world. But Seeger was also aware of a new direction in Dylan's just-released album, *Bringing It All Back Home,* which included electric backup instead of a simple acoustic guitar. At Newport, the citadel of folk music, Dylan came onstage with an electric Fender guitar and an electrically amplified backup blues band. The sound, as he sang "Maggie's Farm," was so loud that the audience could not make out the words.[1]

Seeger was furious. Dylan was making a very public statement about his view of popular music and where it was going, and even though his electrified songs had been played on the radio, Pete was troubled by what seemed a bald and abrasive shift.

Bob Dylan with his electric guitar at Newport on July 25, 1965 (Alice Ochs/Getty Images)

Seeger ran over to the sound man. "Fix the sound so you can hear the words!" he yelled to the man at the controls.

"This is the way they want it," the man shouted back.

"Damn it, "Seeger said, "if I had an axe, I'd cut the cable right now."[2]

Dylan returned to play an acoustic set with his old guitar and harmonica but did not return to Newport again. The musical times were a-changin'.

As the musical world shifted course before Seeger's eyes, he watched the civil rights movement shift course at the same time. He wasn't wholly comfortable with the transition from a peaceful commitment to integration to a more aggressive dedication to Black Power. He had thrown himself into the crusade for equality with a sense of possibility about creating a better multiracial society, but now he was less sure about what contributions he could make as Black Power took hold.

Meanwhile, he was preoccupied with another issue that became the focus of intense national concern. He and other singers lent their voices to a growing chorus of protest as the United States plunged into a guerrilla war halfway around the world in Vietnam. He was soon writing new songs, angrier songs, to galvanize the antiwar movement and energize the effort to bring the conflict to an end.

As Seeger faced these transitions, he went into something of a funk. He wondered what role, if any, remained for him in the increasingly aggressive civil rights movement, and as musical tastes changed, he questioned the direction of his own professional life. Frustrated with changes that were coming so quickly they left him breathless, he dropped his regular column in *Sing Out!* though he did publish a blistering assessment of the contradictions of his career under Toshi's name:

This man is advertised as a singer—but he obviously hasn't much voice.

He is a Yankee but sings southern songs.

He sings old songs, but somehow his meanings are contemporary.

He tries to talk simply, but obviously has a good education and has read widely.

He sings about poor people, though I doubt he is poor himself.

Altogether, he is a very professional amateur.

I would call him a phony, except that I think he is just another modern paradox.[3]

Ever committed to using his music to challenge economic and social injustice, he felt frustrated at having his hands tied.

Gradually Seeger regained his bearing, righted by what he and others regarded as a colossal wrong: the Vietnam War. The roots of the war dated back to French colonial control of Indochina. France conquered this part of Southeast Asia, which includes present-day Vietnam, Laos, and Cambodia, in the middle of the nineteenth century. France remained the dominant colonial power in the region until Japan seized control of it at the start of World War II. Meanwhile, Ho Chi Minh, a Vietnamese nationalist and communist organizer with connections to the Soviet Union, agitated for the independence of his homeland. With Japan's defeat in 1945, he proclaimed the Democratic Republic of Vietnam, but France, after its devastation during the war, was determined to resume control of its colonial empire. Seeking France's support in Europe as the Cold War unfolded, the United States provided substantial economic aid that helped fund what by then was a full-blown anticolonial war in Indochina.

In 1954, Ho Chi Minh's forces defeated the French. An international conference in Geneva, Switzerland, divided Vietnam at the seventeenth parallel, with Ho in control of the north and a government sympathetic to the West in charge in the south. According to the agreement, unification elections would be held in two years. Eager to resist the spread of communism wherever it surfaced, the United States increased its support to the new nation of South Vietnam. By the end of the decade, there were more than 1,500 Americans, many of them military advisers, in the country. That number had swelled to 25,000, 16,000 of them soldiers, at the time of John Kennedy's assassination in 1963.

Kennedy's successor, Lyndon B. Johnson, began large-scale "escalation" of the war, a euphemism coined by the administration to soften what turned out to be a massive increase in the number of troops. Determined not to lose this struggle, which he viewed as a fundamental part of the Cold War, Johnson began to add hundreds of thousands of American troops: 184,000 in 1965, 385,000 in 1966, 485,000 in 1967, and 543,000 by 1968.

Seeger understood what was going on in Southeast Asia years before the war embroiled the United States. "I could remember that way back in 1954, when the French were being defeated in Vietnam, I read in the *Daily Worker*, 'The U.S. establishment will move in now to try to control things there,'" he recalled. "President Eisenhower said, 'The USA must have that tungsten.'"[4] From Seeger's point of view, "the USA was moving into Vietnam illegally."[5]

As the United States waded more deeply into the war, Seeger watched friends and associates speak out. On April 15, 1964, Joan Baez sent in a handwritten letter to the Internal Revenue Service with her tax return. It read:

> Our modern weapons can reduce a man to a piece of dust in a split second, can make a woman's hair fall out or cause her baby to be born a monster. They can kill the part of a turtle's brain that tells him where he is going, so instead of trudging to the ocean he trudges confusedly towards the desert, slowly, blinking his poor eyes, until he finally scorches to death and turns into a shell and some bones.
>
> I am not going to volunteer the 60% of my year's income tax that goes to armaments.[6]

The press publicized this letter and gave it widespread exposure.

Seeger rejected that course of action, but found his own way of giving voice to his protest against military involvement in the war. In 1965, he wrote "King Henry," his first song about Vietnam. Inspired by a letter in a local newspaper, he thought for a time about what to say and finally found his inspiration on a ski trip with his family. He quickly jotted down lyrics that came to mind while on the slopes and in characteristic fashion fit them to an old tune. The song began with events in the sixteenth century as English King Henry VIII launched a bloody war:

> King Henry marched forth, a sword in his hand,
> Two thousand horsemen all at his command;
> In a fortnight the rivers ran red through the land,
> The year fifteen hundred and twenty.

The song was more biting as it turned to the modern day. The third, fourth, and fifth verses came directly from the letter in the newspaper, written by a woman quoting her husband, who had been an American adviser in Vietnam. It told the sad story of the contemporary war in human terms:

> Simon was drafted in '63,
> In '64 sent over the sea;
> Last month this letter he sent to me,
> He said, "You won't like what I'm saying."

> He said, "We've no friends here, no hardly a one,
> We've got a few generals who just want our guns;
> But it'll take more than that if we're ever going to win,
> Why, we'll have to flatten the country."

> "It's my own troops I have to watch out for," he said,
> "I sleep with a pistol right under my head";
> He wrote this last month; last week he was dead,
> And Simon came home in a casket.

The next verse conveyed Seeger's personal sentiments in his own words, with a subtle reference to protesting American policy by withholding taxes:

> I mind my own business, I watch my TV,
> Complain about taxes, but pay anyway;
> In a civilized manner my forefathers betray,
> Who long ago struggled for freedom.[7]

The song got Seeger in trouble, ironically, and typically, the result of an unthinking act of generosity. He was performing a series of concerts in the Soviet Union, singing civil rights and labor songs, encouraging audiences there, as everywhere, to sing along, and pointedly steering clear of the war in Vietnam. A student at Moscow State University, unable to obtain tickets to a regular concert, asked if Pete might put on an extra show for the college crowd. Seeger agreed and was also receptive to the request of Peter Grose, the *New York Times* correspondent in Moscow. In Cold War Russia, Grose confessed, he wasn't allowed on the campus unless he could somehow accompany the singer.

"Sure," Seeger replied, "come along. You can carry my guitar for me."

Seeger followed the same format he had been using in these concerts, filling the bill with labor and civil rights songs. During a question-and-answer period following the concert, one of the Russian students asked, "What kinds of songs are being sung in American universities these days?" Seeger cited the antiwar protest songs of such singers as Phil Ochs and Bob Dylan. Without being asked, he sang "King Henry."[8]

Grose wrote a short article about the concert that first appeared in the Paris edition of an American newspaper and was reprinted in the *New York Times*. The piece ignored the more popular folk songs Seeger had sung and mentioned only "King Henry," under the headline, added by a staffer, "Seeger Sings Anti-American Song in Moscow."

Plainly rankled, Seeger called an editor at the *Times*, who listened to the lyrics, agreed they were not anti-American, and assured him that the headline had been altered in later editions.[9] The subsequent edition, though muted, still skewed the story: "Seeger Critical in Moscow." The lead paragraph highlighted the episode with the statement: "An American folk singer, Pete Seeger, sang a Vietnam protest ballad today before an auditorium filled with Moscow University students." The fairly innocuous story concluded with the observation that "the more familiar folk songs drew more applause than the protest songs," but the damage was done.[10] Seeger, who had survived the attacks by HUAC only a few years earlier, now found himself embroiled in controversy for views at odds with those of mainstream America.

The same song caused further trouble back home. Seeger was scheduled to sing at the high school in his hometown of Beacon, New York, until some citizens, uncomfortable with his radical politics in general and this critical song in particular, gathered seven hundred signatures on a petition to stop the concert. Other residents attacked Seeger directly, lighting several fires on his property. A liberal local doctor told him, "You should cancel the concert. You know this is fascism. You're going to be run out of town."[11]

Pete and Toshi fought back. They gained the support of the Beacon High School students and some local shopkeepers. The elderly and quite conservative owner of a hardware store supported Seeger as a matter of simple democratic decency. "Well, I don't know your politics, young man," he said, "but it's America. You got a right to your opinion."[12] Citing a recent decision by the New York State Supreme Court mandating that public schools renting facilities to any one group must rent to all groups, the head of the local school board declared that he could not legally refuse to allow the concert in the school. Much to his relief, Seeger recalled, "It all turned out pretty well after all. With all this publicity, the high school auditorium was jam-packed, and the folks sang along well."[13]

Despite the best efforts of a growing number of protesters, the country's commitment to the war in Vietnam deepened. As he ran for the presidency in his own right in 1964, Lyndon Johnson posed as the candidate of peace and told voters that he was not "ready for American boys to do the fighting for Asian boys." Over and over he reiterated his intention to "seek no wider war."[14] But the Gulf of Tonkin Resolution that summer, passed in response to questionable reports about attacks by the North Vietnamese on American vessels off the coast of North Vietnam, gave him latitude to do whatever he wanted. It authorized all measures necessary to counter future attacks on U.S. military forces and to assist countries in the region asking for help to defend their freedom. Johnson's campaign was successful and he won the election in a landslide.

But escalation led a protest movement to mushroom. In March 1965, several thousand students and professors at the University of Michigan gathered in what they called a "teach-in" about the war. It was an educational effort in which supporters and opponents of the struggle debated the direction of American policy, explored different sides of the struggle, and provided a model for similar gatherings at colleges and universities around the country. Reasoned debate soon gave way to hot-blooded rallies, more dedicated to criticizing military involvement in Vietnam than weighing both sides.[15] In April of the same year, more than fifteen thousand demonstrators massed at the Washington Monument in the nation's capital to object to the war. Sponsored by the still small radical group Students for a Democratic Society, this was the first national protest against America's military policy in Vietnam.

Escalation continued. In 1965, an early bombing initiative expanded into the massive operation known as "Rolling Thunder," using fragmentation bombs and canisters of napalm, a sticky, jelly-like substance that ignited and clung to human flesh. More and more American soldiers were deployed to Vietnam, and more and more of them came home in caskets. As the public learned about the consequences of bombing raids and saw pictures of burned children, Seeger sometimes seemed to take the devastation personally. Perhaps the fact that his own children were Asian American made him more sensitive to the destruction, even though others were equally horrified by what they saw. "I can't get my mind off Vietnam," he wrote.[16] Once, when he learned of a North Vietnamese child born with a shrapnel tear in her cheek from a bombing raid that predated her birth, he wrote a poem expressing his own anguish:

> You will bear the scar all your life long
> And I, whose only scars are mental ones,
> Must stagger out and tell my countrymen
> What happened.[17]

Disturbed by the contours of U.S. policy, his own long-standing support for the underdog and his near natural skepticism of authority made him sympathetic to the Vietnamese demand for autonomy and independence. The horrors of the war, visible on the nightly television news, now propelled him full bore into the protest movement.

Seeger's contribution, as so often in the past, was to write another song, this one called "Bring 'Em Home." The title served as a refrain appearing after every line. There was no denying the message, which blended what Seeger regarded as true patriotism with a powerful call to end the war:

Pete singing at an antiwar rally at Madison Square Garden in New York City in 1966 (Photo by Diana Jo Davies)

If you love your Uncle Sam,
Bring 'em home, Bring 'em home.
Support our boys in Vietnam,
Bring 'em home, Bring 'em home.

Other verses included such lines as "It'll make our generals sad, I know" and "Show those generals their fallacy."[18] But the refrain remained the centerpiece.

Pete knew he had written better songs. "Not one of my best," he acknowledged. "An editorial in rhyme. I always caution beginning songwriters, 'Beware of editorials in rhyme. Better: Tell a story.' Nevertheless it did its job, got thousands singing that short refrain. And some life-long passions got into the verses."[19]

That same year, Seeger began what became his best song about Vietnam. He saw a photograph in a newspaper of troops wading in the hot, swampy Mekong Delta, and he thought about a song describing the blind tenacity of American leaders and their refusal to alter policy. In a moment of inspiration, he came up with the last line in its entirety, as he put it, "words, tune, rhythm."[20] The line was simple: "Waist deep in the Big Muddy, and the big fool says to push on."[21] This one would be a story, not an editorial in rhyme. All that remained was to come up with a narrative to accompany the refrain. He wrote down the line in a pocket notebook, where it stayed untended for a time. But it haunted him, and over the course of the next several weeks, he finished the song.

"Waist Deep in the Big Muddy" told a sad story of pig-headed stubbornness. Seeger set the story in 1942, but his point was aimed at Vietnam. A platoon of U.S. soldiers on a practice patrol in 1942 is ordered by its captain to ford the Mississippi River, despite the warnings of the sergeant and the men that the river is too deep. The captain refuses to listen and pushes ahead. Each verse told the story of the captain and the men drifting deeper and deeper into the water. It began:

> It was back in nineteen forty-two,
> I was a member of a good platoon.
> We were on maneuvers in-a Loozianna,
> One night by the light of the moon.
>> The captain told us to ford a river.
>> That's how it all begun.
>> We were—knee deep in the Big Muddy,
>> But the big fool said to push on.

The next two verses described the misgivings of the men and the refusal of the captain to listen:

> The Sergeant said, "Sir, are you sure,
> This is the best way back to the base?"
> "Sergeant, go on! I forded this river
> 'Bout a mile above this place.
>> It'll be a little soggy but just keep slogging.
>> We'll soon be on dry ground."
>> We were—waist deep in the Big Muddy
>> And the big fool said to push on.

> The Sergeant said, "Sir with all this equipment
> No man will be able to swim."
> "Sergeant, don't be a Nervous Nellie,"
> The Captain said to him.

"All we need is a little determination;
Men, follow me. I'll lead on."
We were—neck deep in the Big Muddy
And the big fool said to push on.

The outcome, outlined in the next verse, was inevitable:

All at once, the moon clouded over,
We heard a gurgling cry.
A few seconds later, the captain's helmet
Was all that floated by.
    The sergeant said, "Turn around men!"
    I'm in charge from now on."
    And we just made it out of the Big Muddy
    With the captain dead and gone.[22]

The song dealt with World War II, of course, but it clearly concerned
the war in Southeast Asia. "I was thinking about Vietnam," Seeger
confessed. "On the other hand, I purposely decided I would just let
it be an allegory on its own, like the political nursery rhymes."[23]

The connections were clear. President Johnson was fond of
calling critics "Nervous Nellies" when they questioned his policy of escalation and demanded withdrawal from the war. More
to the point, as he hunkered down and refused to shift course
despite growing criticism, he was just like the captain in the song.
Committed to his domestic reform program, which he expansively called the Great Society, he watched as "that bitch of a war,"
in his phrase, eroded its provisions.[24] He felt, he said, like a catfish
that had "grabbed a big juicy worm with a right sharp hook in the
middle of it."[25] Still, once hooked, he refused to let go.

Another verse, the one that made the song controversial,
spelled out the parallels clearly:

Well, I'm not going to point any moral;
I'll leave that for yourself
Maybe you're still walking, you're still talking
You'd like to keep your health.
    But every time I read the papers
    That old feeling comes on;
    We're—waist deep in the Big Muddy and the
    Big fool says to push on.

Seeger said, "[I] sang the song everywhere I could." He was pleased with the response: "At colleges it got an explosive reaction. This was early in '67." Students understood the connections and appreciated the message. Sometimes hecklers interrupted him as he began to sing, but invariably he finished to loud applause. As the draft conscripted more and more young men into military service, threatened students were increasingly receptive to his message. On one occasion they appropriated part of the refrain for their own quite different purpose. After singing in Wisconsin, Seeger spent the night at a professor's home. At lunch the following day his host told him what had happened that morning: "At my first class I started briskly announcing that we had to get cracking the books; from the rear of the room I heard some student mutter, 'The big fool says to push on.'"[26]

Seeger recorded the song for Columbia on an album called *Waist Deep in the Big Muddy and Other Love Songs* before leaving for a concert tour in Germany, Lebanon, and Israel. He returned to the United States as the record was ready to be released. He believed that if this song received ample air time, it could help to turn the nation against the war. John Hammond, the Columbia executive overseeing the recording, agreed to issue it as a single in hopes of having it played to large audiences on AM radio. The plan failed. Despite the chorus of antiwar protests, Columbia Records was not prepared to join the choir. A Columbia staffer in Denver told Seeger what had happened when the recording appeared there: "Pete, I was working in the office of the local distributor for Columbia Records when your single of 'Big Muddy' came in. My boss took one listen and exploded, 'Those guys in New York must be nuts to think I can sell a record like this.' Pete, your record never even left the shelves."[27]

Seeger wanted to play his song on TV. He understood the growing power of the medium and realized that television offered an opportunity to reach masses of people around the country. He had sought to appear on a number of television programs before, but his radical past led TV executives to keep him off the air. In the summer of 1967 the wind changed when Tommy and Dick Smothers, folksinging friends, asked Seeger to appear on their popular television show, *The Smothers Brothers Comedy Hour*. The Smothers Brothers had begun performing as comedians in nightclubs, using their considerable musical talent to poke affectionate fun at folksingers, before gravitating to television. With the show's high ratings, CBS executives wanted to keep the hosts happy. When the network consulted the brothers about possible guests, Tommy replied, "Let us have Seeger."[28]

TV executives and the Smothers Brothers alone could not bring Seeger to the small screen. Procter & Gamble, the soap manufacturer that had sponsored *Hootenanny* several years before and kept Seeger from performing, was again a major advertiser. In August, successful behind-the-scenes negotiations cleared Seeger to perform.

Pete had the support of the press. Breaking the story, the *Los Angeles Times* called the impending performance an "important event" and declared that it was "the glimmer of light at the end of what must seem to Seeger like an endless black tunnel."[29] The *New York Times* reminded readers that Seeger had not sung on network TV since 1950, when he appeared with the Weavers. It repeated the story of his conviction, and its subsequent reversal, for refusing to answer HUAC questions and noted the controversy that occurred as a result of his blacklisting by the *Hootenanny* show. The paper disclosed the ABC network's demand during that dispute that "it would consider allowing him to appear if he signed an affidavit regarding his political affiliation," and observed that "Seeger refused to do so on Constitutional grounds." CBS, it went on, had not asked him to sign any oaths or statements. In an editorial a week and a half after the first story, the paper declared, "It is time to nail the lid on the blacklist coffin."[30]

In early September, Seeger went to Hollywood to tape the program, pleased by the course of events. He believed that if he could only sing his song to a large enough audience he could persuade people to demand an end to the war. "I felt history was being made," he said. "And when you stop to realize—it was. The more President Johnson got into the war, the more opposition there was, far beyond the narrow left or pacifist wing.... All of a sudden here was a breach in the wall of prime time, a very dangerous thing as far as the establishment was concerned."[31] Earlier, he had contemplated buying TV time on his own to sing "Waist Deep in the Big Muddy." Now that was unnecessary. He had an audience waiting and the confidence to believe that he could convince those watching to join together to stop the war.

In the videotaping session that preceded the TV show, Seeger sang several songs, including old favorites like "Wimoweh" and "John Brown's Body," and concluded, as he told the Smothers Brothers he would, with "Waist Deep in the Big Muddy." Staffers took the tape to New York for CBS officials to check before it was to be shown a few days later.

When the program aired, Seeger and others were appalled. Without a word of warning or explanation, "'Big Muddy' had been cut out of the tape." The excision was as blunt as it was evident: "One moment I had a guitar in my hand; a second later I had a banjo in my hand—it was an obvious cut."[32]

Pete on The Smothers Brothers Comedy Hour (Collection of Pete and Toshi Seeger)

As Seeger sought an explanation, he spun things with characteristic generosity. "It's perfectly possible that some clever person at CBS said, 'No, don't let him sing his song now,'" he later observed. "'Let's build up publicity and let him sing it in January.' It's theoretically possible. On the other hand I think more likely they said, 'That's just the kind of godamn song we knew he'd try and sing. Well, we've got to stop it somehow—scissor it out.' The editor said, 'How do I do it?' 'Oh,' they said, 'find a way.' So the poor editor might have said, 'Well, I'll do it the most awkward way, so everybody knows it's been scissored out.'"[33] The rationalizations hardly reduced the singer's frustration. The fact remained that the song Seeger wanted to sing most of all had not appeared on national TV.

The CBS censorship was puzzling. Columbia Records, part of the larger corporation that included the television network, featured "Waist Deep in the Big Muddy" on Seeger's latest album. Why, *Newsweek* wondered, would it then turn around and remove the song from the air?[34] Other publications were even more critical. *Variety,* the entertainment industry outlet, headlined a front-page story "'Big Muddy' in CBS-TV's Eye: Slip Seeger's Number for Anti LBJ Slant." The *New York Times,* which highlighted Seeger in its "Television This Week," ran its own pointed headline after the debacle: "Seeger Accuses CBS over Song."[35] Trying to be diplomatic despite his irritation, Seeger telegrammed a CBS vice president to say that he was not charging CBS with malfeasance. But he added, "Do feel strongly that radio and TV communications should allow audiences to judge for themselves. The best censor is that little knob on the set."[36]

The Smothers Brothers also spoke out. As Seeger recalled, they complained, "CBS is censoring our best jokes; they censored

Seeger's best song."[37] They didn't stop there. "We definitely plan to have Seeger back," Tommy told reporters, "and he's probably gonna want to sing 'Big Muddy' again. Maybe we'll sing it with him."[38]

Several months later, CBS executives decided to allow Seeger to sing "Waist Deep in the Big Muddy" on the air. With but a day's notice, Pete flew to California, taped the song again, and watched it on the program in February 1968, along with some seven million other viewers. Only a network station in Detroit cut the song. But CBS had the last word. The next year, without explanation, it canceled the Smothers Brothers show. The musicians never learned whether Seeger or his song had anything to do with it.

The Smothers Brothers may have disappeared from television, but the war in Vietnam flooded into American homes on nightly news broadcasts with relentless regularity. In January 1968, just before Seeger sang on CBS, the Viet Cong (South Vietnamese guerrillas) and North Vietnamese regulars launched a huge coordinated military offensive at the start of Tet, the lunar New Year. Invading a hundred South Vietnamese cities and towns, they even attacked the U.S. Embassy in Saigon. The war, television screens plainly showed, was far from over.

Though the attacks were repelled and enemy casualties high, the Tet offensive demonstrated that, where the war was concerned, perceptions trumped reality. And perceptions fueled protest around the United States. College campuses exploded with marches, rallies, sit-ins and chants of "Hey, hey, LBJ / How many kids did you kill today?" In the March New Hampshire Democratic presidential primary, the antiwar candidate Senator Eugene McCarthy, a virtual unknown, received a stunning 42 percent of the vote, only slightly less than Johnson himself. The president, who desperately wanted to run for reelection in November, realized that the opposition to his candidacy would fracture the nation.[39] In a televised speech later that month he declared, "I shall not seek, and I will not accept, the nomination of my party for another term as your President."[40]

Relief at Johnson's willingness to step aside turned to horror five days later with the assassination of Martin Luther King, Jr., in Memphis, Tennessee. Television showed the desperate rioting that erupted in many American cities out of blind fury at the senseless killing. Exactly two months later, on June 4, the charismatic Robert F. Kennedy, brother of the slain president and now an antiwar candidate for the presidency, was shot after his victory in the California Democratic primary. Again television carried story after story about the murder, nurturing the public frustration Seeger had long thought possible, even if he wasn't in the spotlight himself.

Like millions of Americans, Seeger was troubled, even depressed, by the chaos that threatened to rip the country apart in 1968. On one occasion, he wrote in his journal, "I feel like I'm on a ship and we're going down the river. There's a big crew and we're having a party. Everybody is singing and dancing and having a marvelous time. And the word comes in that there is a huge waterfall ahead. I go up and try to tell everybody that we had better stop and get the ship turned around before we go over the falls. But everybody is so busy singing and dancing that they won't listen to me." Like Cassandra, the tragic Greek heroine with the power of dark prophecy, he faced the curse of warnings ignored.

Seeger's feelings of hopelessness peaked publicly when he appeared on Steve Allen's television variety show in 1968. Singing the old standard "It Takes a Worried Man," he stopped abruptly after two verses, saying simply, "I can't sing this song."[41] Somehow, he told friends, he had lost his spirit. When he and Toshi joined a poor people's campaign in Washington, D.C., he wondered if he made any difference. In the past, he had loved singing Woody Guthrie's classic "This Land Is Your Land." Now, according to Bernice Johnson Reagon, a friend from civil rights days who founded the singing group Sweet Honey in the Rock, "it felt like he didn't know *what* to sing ... he was not sure what his function was."[42]

Seeger remained frustrated as the Republican Richard Nixon won the presidency that year. Though Nixon claimed to have a secret plan to end the war in Vietnam, in fact no such plan existed. But he did reduce tension at home by Vietnamization, replacing U.S. soldiers with Vietnamese troops. At the same time, his insistence on gaining "peace with honor" led him in the opposite direction, widening the war by bombing campaigns that pulverized the landscape and killed countless soldiers and civilians in both North and South Vietnam.

In mid-November 1969, an estimated half million people gathered in Washington, D.C., to protest the war. Pete and Toshi joined activists from around the country in a massive demonstration on the Mall. When Seeger stepped up to the microphone on the stage, he and the civil rights activist Fred Kirkpatrick had trouble getting the crowd to sing in rhythm together. The "audience was just too big," Seeger recalled, "and by the time the rhythm got back there a quarter mile, it came back to us a beat late."[43] His antiwar song "Bring 'Em Home" failed to move the crowd.

Glancing over at the woman who was timing participants with a stopwatch to make sure they stayed on schedule, Pete held up an index finger as if to ask, "OK to sing one more song?" When she nodded yes, he decided to gamble with a short refrain by John Lennon and Yoko Ono. Pete had heard the words only three days before and sung the line only once. The simple tune and its message stuck with him: "All we are saying, is Give Peace a Chance."[44] Seeger later noted, "That's all there is to it. A song only seven seconds long." The two performers sang it over and over. After about thirty seconds, other people joined in, thousands of people, then tens of thousands, and finally hundreds of thousands. The trio

Huge antiwar rally on the Mall in Washington, D.C., in November 1969 (Photo by Theodore Hetzel, Theodore Hetzel Collection [Box 2], Swarthmore College Peace Collection)

Peter, Paul and Mary came up to the left of the podium and Mitch Miller, a choir leader who had popularized the sing-along format on television, jumped up on the right, waving his arms to help the crowd keep time.

Looking out from the stage, Seeger was overwhelmed. It was, he recalled, "like a huge ballet, flags, banners, signs, would move to the right for three beats (one measure) and then left for the next measure. Parents had children on their shoulders, swaying in rhythm." After five or six minutes of singing and swaying, Seeger and his partners "let it end softly as in a gospel church when a rhythm has been sung till no one can add more."[45] The moment, sweet with the voices of many singing as one, brought people together as almost nothing else could, united in the fervent hope that peace would get its chance.

The moment, sweet as it was, did not last. Protestors might raise their voices in song, might lift their hearts in hope, but their voices fell on deaf ears and their hopes for peace never had a chance. Nixon was determined to push on. The war dragged on for the duration of his first term, until finally, in early 1973, a peace treaty allowed the United States to leave. Two years later, in 1975, the North Vietnamese reunified the country on their own terms. Helicopters on the roof of the U.S. Embassy in Saigon rescued the fortunate few, leaving all the rest of the South Vietnamese to face the North Vietnamese on their own.

Like most critics, Seeger was relieved to see the war end. It had been a bitter, brutal struggle, but the final result vindicated his faith in the power of critics, particularly those singing songs, to make a difference in the political arena. He knew that countless others spoke out, protested, and forced political leaders to listen. But he always believed that songs could help, and music did play a part in the antiwar campaign. It brought people together with a sense of common purpose, focused attention on disastrous policy decisions, and provided hope that masses of Americans singing together could force political change. Music helped highlight the passion of the movement. The tragedy was that more than fifty thousand Americans and millions of Vietnamese died before the conflict came to an end.

Even after the war, Seeger retained his admiration for Ho Chi Minh, the nationalist revolutionary who led North Vietnam after a partition of the country in 1954. Seeger never met Ho, who died several years before the singer visited Southeast Asia in 1972. Even so, he venerated the homespun hero held in such affection by so many Vietnamese. On his own trip to Vietnam, he wore sandals "made out of tires with rubber straps from the inner tubes of tires...just like Uncle Ho...the kind of sandals he wore. He didn't go around with the uniform on like Mao Zedong did or Stalin did or other great leaders are supposed to. What a guy. What a guy."[46]

Ho was, Seeger once said, "a poet, a storyteller with a great sense of humor." So was Seeger, who was fond of telling a story that he and Toshi heard on their 1972 Vietnam trip, about Ho stopping at an army camp. Finding officers in the front, non-commissioned officers in the middle, and enlisted men at the back of the room, "Ho immediately goes to the rear of the hall, shouts 'about face' and gives a short speech to the effect that the rank-and-file are the most important part of the army, the country, the world." Ho, he said, was one of his "all-time heroes."[47]

As the war ended, Seeger was satisfied with the result, though his views about Ho Chi Minh and his revolutionary leadership were clearly out of step with the attitudes of many Americans. While some people deplored the loss of a struggle they believed the United States should have won, Seeger put doubt and depression behind him and became fully involved in another cause that revived his faith in the possibility of progress and the power of song.

· *Six* ·

"Sailing Down My Golden River"

∞

Looking down from his hillside home, Seeger could see the Hudson River rolling south toward Manhattan. He loved the cabin he built with his own hands and the river that flowed beneath it. The thick forest reminded him of a childhood spent tromping through the woods, camping out, exploring the outdoors. "I luff the woods," he once told his father.[1] Even now, in his early forties, with his long legs and strong constitution, he still delighted in hiking across the land. But as he looked down at the river, he liked what he saw less and less. The water was filling up with chemical waste and sludge from factories and sewage plants. Once clear and blue, the Hudson was turning murky and brown. Cleaning it up became his focus as he threw himself into the fledgling environmental movement.

Even before the war in Vietnam ended, Seeger found himself sympathizing with the efforts of environmental activists. Ever the radical, he became outraged at those who spoiled the natural environment in pursuit of personal gain. "I've been living with this issue for 82 years," he observed several decades later. "Do we organize society around the golden rule or be ruled by money?"[2] Eagerly he began to play a role in another of the crusades that shaped the contours of his life.

Environmental activism was nothing new. Twice before in the twentieth century, conservation advocates had launched campaigns to protect the nation's resources. In the early years of the century, Theodore Roosevelt helped create a system of national forests and wildlife preserves. During the New Deal of the 1930s, Franklin Roosevelt drew on his rural roots in Hyde Park, New York, and established programs like the Civilian Conservation Corps to build wilderness paths and trails and renew America's system of forests and parks.

The third great wave of environmental awareness began several decades later. In 1962, the naturalist Rachel Carson warned the public about the dangers of pesticide poisoning and environmental pollution in her landmark book *Silent Spring*. Highlighting the devastating impact of pest-killing chemicals such as DDT, she documented the disastrous side effects that ran through the entire food chain. "The most alarming of all man's assaults upon the environment is the contamination of air, earth, rivers, and sea with dangerous and even lethal materials," she wrote. "This pollution is for the most part irrecoverable; the chain of evil it initiates not only in the world that must support life but in living tissues is for the most part irreversible."[3] Her book sparked national attention about the need to preserve the natural environment. It also led President Johnson to push for new measures to limit air and water pollution as part of his Great Society program.

Seeger could not have been happier with this turn of environmental events. "I've been a nature nut all my life," he later recalled. As the young camper who once built a tepee in the woods grew older, he found he liked "to read about nature just for the fun of it, whether it was monarch butterflies in Mexico" or creatures elsewhere in the world.[4] In the early 1950s he read the selection from Carson's *The Sea around Us* that appeared in the *New Yorker*. Later, in 1963, like so many other Americans, he devoured her blockbuster *Silent Spring*. It was, he observed, "a very quiet little book," but it packed a punch.[5] He realized, "It might be before we bomb each other off the face of the earth we may poison each other off the face of the earth."[6]

For Seeger, the book was "a turning point." It made him revise his political and social priorities: "I'd been a nature nut. Age 15 and 16, I put all that behind me, figuring the main job to do was to help the meek inherit the earth, assuming that when they did the foolishness of the private profit system would be put to an end." But now, he understood, things had changed: "In the early '60s I realized that the world was being turned into a poisonous garbage dump. By the time the meek inherited it, it might not be worth inheriting." He became what he called an "econik" and began reading books by environmental scholars such as the ecologist Barry Commoner and the entomologist Paul Ehrlich.[7]

Silent Spring came at the right moment for Seeger. He was just beginning to spend more time outdoors, particularly on the Hudson River near his home. And he found himself intrigued with sailing. As a boy, he had built wooden sailboats in his father's tool shop. Now he wanted to sail himself, especially after he gave a concert on Cape Cod and a teenager took him out in a small boat and showed him what to do. "I realized that there was something almost magical about it," he said. "The wind and the waves—you play a game with them." He loved the idea of tacking back and forth to reach a desired destination: "The wind can be coming from the north, but if you slant your sails right you can go northwest, then northeast, then northwest, then northeast, and use the very power of the north wind to inch your way north." Moving that way, he added, "is good politics too."[8]

As the years passed, Seeger's interest in sailing grew. Fellow folksinger Jack Elliot sparked his interest by showing him a children's book titled *We Didn't Mean to Go to Sea*. Seeger took the next step on his own and bought a boat, "a little plastic bathtub of a boat," he recalled: "[I] took my family out in it."[9] He loved to feel the wind whistling by as he glided through the water. "Such poetry!" he enthused, until one awful day: "Sailing on the Hudson, I saw lumps of toilet waste floating past me."[10] The pollution came, he understood, from corporate interests unwilling to spend the money to dispose of waste in a different way. He was so struck by the contrast between "private affluence and public squalor" that he wrote a song.[11] Called "Sailing Up My Dirty Stream," it captured his love of the river and his hope that perhaps someday it would be clean again:

> Sailing up my dirty stream
> Still I love it and I'll keep the dream
> That someday, though maybe not this year
> My Hudson River will once again run clear.
> She starts high in the mountains of the north
> Crystal clear and icy trickles forth

> With just a few floating wrappers of chewing gum
> Dropped by some hikers to warn of things to come.

Another verse was even more graphic:

> Down the valley one million toilet chains
> Find my Hudson so convenient a place to drain.[12]

Hardly an inspired effort, it reflected his frustration with the casual contamination that was ruining the river.

Despite the filth and contamination, he kept returning to the water, usually by himself, and found that drifting down the river made him feel peaceful. Hardly an expert sailor, he capsized his boat more than once, which meant he was in even closer contact with the sludge. Still, he kept on sailing. It was worth it; he found the renewal he sought from the river he loved. He recalled one occasion: "I was learning to sail, and spent my first night alone on the river, seeing the evening light go from golden to rose, to purple, to night. Made up a tune as I went along, and only realized a month later that I'd swiped the first part of the melody from one of my favorite Christmas carols, 'Deck the Halls.'" He called this far more lyrical song "Sailing Down My Golden River." It conveyed the quiet passion that he felt on the water:

> Sailing down my golden river
> Sun and water all my own
>   Yet I was never alone.
> Sun and water, old life-givers
> I'll have them where'er I roam
>   And I was not far from home.
>
> Sunlight glancing on the water
> Life and death are all my own
>   And I was never alone.

Life to raise my sons and daughters
Golden sparkles in the foam
And I was not far from home.

Sailing down this winding highway
Travelers from near and far
Yet I was never alone.
Exploring all the little by-ways
Sighting all the distant stars
Yet I was not far from home.[13]

Seeger had doubts about the song. "Like 'Where Have All the Flowers Gone?'" he said, "I wrote it and didn't think it was such a good song. I never sang it." Then he heard Don McLean, a folk-singer friend, singing it in harmony with another singer. "Where did you learn that?" Seeger asked.

"Oh, we heard you sing it."

"Well, gee," Seeger replied, "that's beautiful."

"Yeah, it's a good song."

"I had made it up," Seeger said, "and I was too embarrassed to sing it."[14] Now it became part of his repertoire.

As he was learning to sail, he became intrigued with even bigger boats. Victor Schwartz, an artist friend, told him about ships with seventy-foot booms that once sailed on the river. Pete could hardly believe that such behemoths glided down the Hudson. "Oh, don't give me that," he said. "There never was a sloop that big, except an America's Cup racer."

"No, I've got a book all about them," Schwartz said. "I'll lend it to you." The dog-eared volume, published in 1908, was *Sloops of the Hudson* by William Verplanck and Moses Collyer. "Before we die, we want to put down what we can remember of these sloops," they wrote, "because they were the most beautiful boats we ever knew, and they will never be seen again."[15] The book contained stories and pictures of the sixty- to ninety-foot boats with hundred-foot masts that once made their way up and down the river. Seeger was fascinated. "It wasn't great literature," he acknowledged, "but I loved it."[16] And it led him to write a meandering poem that conjured up the river as it once was.

> Four hundred plied the river in 1860
> Often built in small yards, in towns like
> Cornwall, Marlborough, New Hamburg.

Quoting from the book, he wrote about 250-pound sturgeon leaping in the air, suddenly landing on the deck of a small boat. And he deplored the sloops' demise.[17]

Seeger started to dream about doing something he'd never done before: building a large boat like those majestic ships of the past. At the same time he finally recognized the need to improve relations with his Hudson River Valley neighbors. His ties to those who lived along the river had always been tenuous, especially as he traveled. Though he cut down trees for a community school and Toshi served on the PTA, those endeavors meant little to local residents suspicious of the gaunt radical who'd had more than a few brushes with the law.

As Seeger's national and international reputation soared, his local reputation sank. His neighbors continued to think of him as a kook. The more conservative ones mobilized—unsuccessfully—to keep him from singing in the local high school. Even though he was able to perform, the episode left him shaken. As he wrote in 1968 to the entertainers Ossie Davis and Ruby Dee, "One of the weaknesses in my own work, and probably the work of many an intellectual, is that I may have friends all around the world, but in my own neighborhood, I am in a very weak position, and can be knocked down by anyone who wants to tell a few lies about me."[18] Old friends from his civil rights days offered sage advice: it was time to go to work in his own backyard.

The more he thought about it, the more he wanted to build a boat and perhaps use it to highlight the need to clean up the river. "Wouldn't it be fun to build one of these sloops?" he asked Jack Elliot and other friends.[19] Impulsively, at midnight in September 1965, he typed a seven-page letter to his friend Victor Schwartz, suggesting such a project. "One way to see if a pipe dream has any practicality is to get it down on paper," he wrote. "So I'm writing you now with the most grandiose and ambitious plan. It will make our wives groan. It probably will never get beyond the paper stage, but here goes."[20] Then came his proposal. "Why don't we get a gang of people together and build a life-size replica of a Hudson River sloop?" he suggested. "It would probably cost $100,000, but if we got enough people together we could raise it." As other causes and concerts preoccupied him, he forgot about the letter.

Four months later, he met his friend on a railroad platform. "When are we going to get started on that boat?" Schwartz asked.

"What boat?"

"You wrote me a letter!"

"Oh, that's as foolish as saying let's build a canoe and paddle to Tahiti."

"Well, I've passed your letter up and down the commuter train; we've got a dozen people who don't think it's foolish."

"Hm. Maybe if there are enough nuts, we just might do it."[21]

Friends thought the idea was absurd. Elliot told him, "The boat would cost $100,000 at the minimum, and require a large crew." He asked the essential question: "Where are you going to get that kind of money?" Mary Travers, of the Peter, Paul and Mary trio, was more blunt. "You're out of your mind," she said.[22]

Seeger refused to be blown off course. Arlo Guthrie, his fellow folksinger and the son of his friend Woody, understood: "Pete wants to clean up the river. Everybody says, 'Pete can't clean up the river. River's too big. Not enough people. Nobody's going to help you.' That didn't stop Pete."[23] Seeger believed that he could get enough people to work together to raise the funds. The sloop could be more than a magnificent ship; it could bridge the gap between "wealthy yachtsmen and kids from the ghettos, church members and atheists."[24] Music had always been the instrument he'd used to bring people together. Now, perhaps, a ship filled with song could do the same.

Pete and Toshi set out to raise the money they needed. At just that moment, chance set Alexander Saunders, a businessman who ran a metals business in neighboring Cold Spring, in their path. Saunders approached Seeger to ask if the singer might give a fund-raising concert on behalf of a group called Scenic Hudson, which was working to stop a water power plant from being built on nearby Storm King Mountain. Seeger agreed, but when Saunders went to the board of directors for approval, he found that Seeger's HUAC hearing and his subsequent contempt conviction frightened more conservative colleagues. He reported their response to Seeger: "Oh don't touch Seeger with a ten-foot pole. If we have anything to do with him, we will be tarred with the same brush!" Saunders did not hide his disappointment. "Sorry they turned me down," he said, "but I'd like to hear some music so maybe we can raise some money for something else." Schwartz piped up, "Pete and I are talking about trying to raise money to build a Hudson River sloop."[25]

Saunders was intrigued, and a month or two later, Seeger found himself singing before 160 people on the back lawn of the Saunderses' home in the town of Garrison. They passed the hat around and raised $160. Not much, but it was a start. More important than the money was the commitment to start an organization to pursue the project. During the concert intermission, about fifteen interested people gathered in the Saunderses' living room and agreed to establish what they called Hudson River Sloop Restoration, Inc., though as Seeger recalled, no one really knew what it would do. One of the founding members was an attorney, and he arranged for the fledgling organization to apply for tax-exempt status.

The first fund-raising concert featured Seeger and Schwartz singing sea chanties. Playing a guitar, swapping verses with an idol, "having the greatest time of my life," Schwartz could hardly believe his good fortune. "I know so many people, so many kids I've run into," he thought, "who would give their right arm to be doing what I'm doing, standing on a platform, singing with this man....I just can't believe I'm that lucky."[26] As Schwartz's mind wandered, Seeger leaned over and whispered that he had just sung the verse Schwartz was now singing. No matter: the crowd applauded, and the concert brought in about $5,000. A festival

Hudson River Sloop Restoration, Inc.

presents

Pete Seeger

Tuesday, November 21, 8 p.m.
Glens Falls High School Auditorium
Donation $2.50

"By any standard, Pete Seeger is a giant of the modern cultural scene . . . the real father of the folk music movement which is such an integral part of the American setting in the 1960's."

Jack Gould, New York Times

The Editor of the Adirondack Community College paper said: "One of the most enjoyable evenings we have spent was up in Granville the night of the Pete Seeger concert. It was tremendous."

Tickets on sale at . . . .

Triad Music Center, Glens Falls, Blue Jack Music Store, Glens Falls, Victor Secci Barber Shop, Granville, Cafe Lena, Saratoga Springs, Mr. Music, Ballston Spa, Van Curler Music Store, Albany.

Mail orders:
Write Hudson River Sloop Restoration, Inc., P.O. Box 205, Salem, N.Y. Send check or money order to Sloop Restoration and include self-addressed and stamped envelope.

Poster for a fund-raising concert for the Clearwater (Collection of Pete and Toshi Seeger)

the next year raised about $10,000. The following year, 1968, fea-
tured Arlo Guthrie as the guest star, and this time six thousand
people showed up. The festival raised still more money along
with some substantial pledges.

Meanwhile, Seeger was busy canvassing wealthy residents of the
area. Never comfortable with small talk, he went to countless cocktail
parties and barbecues, the kinds of gatherings he managed to avoid
in the past. He learned what he had to do by watching others. When
Jimmy Collier, a folksinger friend from the civil rights movement,
came to Beacon, he greeted people easily, had a beer with locals, and
invited them down to the waterfront. "It was a real lesson," Seeger
said. "Here I thought of myself as somebody who knew political
organizing, but I didn't know it at all. Because all I had to do was
come in and sing a song. Other people had to do the dirty work."[27]
As always, Toshi played a central part, keeping the new organization
on track with attention to all of the promotional details.

As the fund-raising continued, members of the group needed
to figure out how to build a boat. Seeger, the driving force and
chairman of the board, wrote to various libraries to see if plans for
an old sloop existed. The only response came from a young man
at Connecticut's Mystic Seaport, an open-air museum depicting
nineteenth-century New England life. He had a set of plans and
invited Seeger to Mystic to examine them. Together they located
Cyrus Hamlin, a naval architect who had been designing boats
for decades. He was fascinated with the project, and in the end
charged Hudson River Sloop Restoration, Inc. only $6,000 for
drawing up plans that should have cost $60,000.[28]

Once they had their own plans, Seeger and the group had to
find a way to build the boat. Estimates ran to $300,000, clearly

prohibitive. But Harvey Gamage, a boatbuilder in South Bristol, Maine, offered to construct the sloop for about $120,000. He was anxious to get started. "Wait a minute," Seeger said. "We only have $30,000. We don't know how we're going to get the rest." Gamage had an answer: "Well, you'll find when the keel is laid, the money comes in quicker."[29] The group followed Gamage's advice and laid the keel on October 18, 1968. Toshi sprinkled it with a bottle of Hudson River water.

The boat took shape quickly. When not raising money, Seeger himself went to Maine to help out at the shipyard. He had always enjoyed physical activity. Instead of felling trees, he painted the boat's weights and set them in place, working alongside much younger volunteers as devoted as he to the project.

On his fiftieth birthday, Seeger decided to celebrate by growing a beard. When he was with the Weavers, his manager told him that he and the others should look conventional, so he shaved his face clean and kept it that way in the years that followed. "Now's my chance," he said to himself. "Nobody is around to say no, so I'll try it." At a time when long hair and beards were common largely among the young, workers in the shipyard were taken aback by the fuzzy-faced singer. When Seeger told them he was going to get a wrench in the shop, one of them replied, "Better pick up a razor too."[30] But the beard was as liberating as the building project and put Seeger in an expansive mood.

As the boat neared completion, Pete wondered what to call it. Nearly half the members of the organization wanted to name it *Heritage* and thus turn it into a historical project rather than something that smacked of what they called "environmental confrontation." Instead, they argued, "let the boat be a graceful symbol of the past."[31] By a narrow vote, the name *Clearwater* triumphed, reflecting the purpose of the boat: to clean up the river.

The christening came seven months later, on May 17, 1969. The completed sloop, which ended up costing about $140,000, was 106 feet long, with a 108-foot mast. It could sleep fifteen and included a captain's cabin and a mess for cooking. It looked just like one of the nineteenth-century ships Seeger and Schwartz had imagined, though its sails were made of Dacron, a synthetic fiber, instead of the traditional canvas and it had electricity and an engine.

There were complicated questions about just how the boat could be used. Construction proceeded before all the necessary funds had been raised, and members of Hudson River Sloop Restoration, Inc., hoped that they could use the completed sloop to collect the balance of the bill. But how exactly could they use the *Clearwater* to spin gold?

At least their intentions were becoming clearer. Three months after the launch, in an article in *Look,* the nationally circulating picture magazine, Seeger described what he foresaw: "The basic idea is to take a beautiful old boat and sail it up and down a still-beautiful river, stopping at every town and city. The waterfront is public property; we'll hold a party, free for everybody, and we mean everybody. Young and old. Black and white. Rich and poor. Male and female. Square and hip. Hairy and shaven. Country and city."

Seeger was describing the same ideals that guided his crusades for the past thirty years. As ever, he sought a more inclusive society in which a variety of voices could be heard. At the same time he wanted all of these people working together to focus attention

SING OUT!
THE FOLK SONG MAGAZINE
VOLUME 19/NUMBER 2   JULY/AUGUST, 1969 $1.00

BILL MONROE   FRED McDOWELL
HARRY SMITH
PLUS 11 NEW AND
TRADITIONAL SONGS

Sloop.

Sing Out! *Magazine drawing of the sloop after its launch* (© The Sing Out! Corporation, all rights reserved)

on the needs of the river. "What's the message?" he asked. "Put simply, we want people to learn to love their river again." In his mind, there was an even larger purpose at work. "I must say I think that the messages will go a lot further than that," he wrote. "You see, everything in the world is tied together. You try to clean up a river, and soon you have to work on cleaning up the society." Ever critical of abuses in the land he loved, he went on, "Only the most starry-eyed, head-in-the-clouds optimist could assume that the U.S.A. and the world can continue on their present course for long. I'm thinking of polluted air and oceans, of bulldozed forest land, of the population bomb, of people vs. property, of the violence-military crisis. Perhaps the sewer running past your door is as good a place to start on the clean-up job as any."[32]

Seeger understood the challenges that lay ahead. He noted with some bemusement, "It's probably the first time a banjo picker has been chairman of the board."[33] He dreamed of letting people board the ship for free. He wanted musicians as crew members, singing their way up and down the river. But he also recognized that the sloop needed a full-time captain, licensed by the Coast Guard, and a crew whose members knew what they were doing

The Clearwater *at sail* (Collection of Pete and Toshi Seeger)

to keep the ship afloat. And so he supported hiring the necessary professional staff.

After its launch, the *Clearwater* sailed forty miles to Portland, Maine, where the musicians put on their first concert. Townspeople "came down to the water's edge," Seeger rhapsodized, "to look at one of the world's most beautiful boats, a symphony of curves, especially under sail."[34] Homemade food accompanied homemade music. Other concerts followed. By the time the sloop reached New York's City's East River after a thirty-seven-day maiden voyage, the *Clearwater* had raised $27,000 from these performances.

Pete by the boom of the Clearwater (Collection of Pete and Toshi Seeger)

As the ship pulled into New York Harbor, drivers on the Triborough and Queensborough Bridges slowed to watch it sailing by. Tugboats drew close for a better look. Mayor John V. Lindsay boarded the boat as it reached Manhattan and took the tiller for a time. Seeger was delighted, despite the unending glare of the media. "The price of liberty is eternal publicity. And we're getting it," he said in a comment that appeared in the *New York Times* as the "Quote of the Day."[35]

Not all onlookers appreciated the sloop's environmental message. At the launching, some threw beer cans into the water, until one member of the *Clearwater* team jumped up and shouted, "In view of the purpose for which this boat is built, let's stop throwing trash in the water."[36] In the ship's second season, the *Clearwater* docked at Cold Spring, once a hotbed of Ku Klux Klan activity. There were rumors of impending trouble, but Seeger was not worried. "Well, we got away with it last summer," he said. "Let's not back out now." As it turned out, no one backed down. The Mid-Hudson Philharmonic played a Haydn symphony to an audience of five hundred people, but trouble erupted when Seeger came on stage to offer a word of thanks just before the orchestra performed the last piece. About fifteen drunken individuals rose, unfurled small American flags, and yelled, "Throw the Commies out." They held up a banner in front of the stage that read "Stop Pollution, Get Rid of Pete."[37] After playing the short scheduled selection, the orchestra conductor called for the "Star-Spangled Banner" in an effort to avoid trouble. But that evening, after Seeger left, someone cut the sloop's mooring line.

Pete took enormous pride in the success of the *Clearwater*. He loved sailing on the ship and stopping at various towns and villages for fund-raising concerts. He was even more pleased just

to sail on the river with musicians serving as crew members singing whenever the spirit moved them.

Over the next several years, Seeger wrote song after song, some
alone, some with others, celebrating the river, the sloop, and the
swelling campaign to solve the problems of pollution. In 1969 he
contributed a verse to the "Ballad of the Sloop *Clearwater*":

> Now, the Sloop is gone, once again I'm ready
>   to watch that river rot
> While others feel the skyfire, and others hug
>   the shot.
> But some folks in town are up and around
>   asking, "What-how-why-and-when!"
> Ever since that Sloop Clearwater
>   came sailing 'round the bend.
> Ever since that Sloop Clearwater
>   came sailing 'round the bend.[38]

Four years later, he wrote the lovely, lyrical words to "Of Time
and Rivers Flowing," setting them to an old German Christmas
carol melody, "Lo, How a Rose E're Blooming":

> Of time and rivers flowing
> The seasons make a song
> And we who live beside her
> Still try to sing along
>   Of rivers, fish, and men
>   And the season still a-coming
>   When she'll run clear again.[39]

In 1977, true to the radical political convictions that had guided
him all his life, he contributed to a seventh verse of Bill Steele's
playful but pointed song "Garbage":

In Mister Thompson's fac-to-ry
   they're making plastic Christmas trees
Complete with silver tinsel and a geodesic stand
The plastic's mixed in giant vats
   from some con-glom-er-ation that's
Been piped from deep within the earth
   or strip mined from the land.
         And if you question anything they say,
         "Why, don't you see
         It's ab-so-lute-ly needed for the
         e-co-no-my," oh
Garbage (garbage, garbage)
   Garbage! (garbage, garbage).[40]

While Seeger sang, the *Clearwater* volunteers were defining their role in environmental education—and the cost. Teaching was the goal, but large insurance bills and salaries for the trained staff members required by law left them desperate for money. Concerts and river festivals provided some cash but never enough for all they needed. So they looked elsewhere and found help from an unexpected source: the government.

With a grant from New York State they took Beacon school-children onboard the ship to instruct them about the river.[41] One of the crew members developed the show-and-tell pattern that emerged. As Seeger recalled, "Fifty kids pile out of a bus, and they're divided into five groups. When the boat is sailing ten are sent to the starboard side and learn to put a net into the water to catch some fish while ten are sent to the port side to put some water under a microscope. 'Hey, what's those wiggly things?' A volunteer crew member…says, 'That's called plankton. Plankton is for fish what grass is for cows.' The murkiness in the river is not all pollution; much of it is plankton. And so we found that schools loved for their kids to go out."[42] Another group took the tiller, and still another went below to see the modern equipment that ran the ship. Every twenty minutes or so, the groups changed places.

With the war in Vietnam widening as the *Clearwater* was launched, Seeger remained a lightning rod for criticism. He frequently sang antiwar as well as environmental songs at fund-raising concerts. Protest songs often alienated conservatives, some of whom were strong supporters of environmental causes. A few *Clearwater* officials, moreover, refused to take Seeger seriously. "As long as Seeger's connected with this project, it'll never get

Toshi and Pete at a Clearwater *revival* (Collection of Pete and Toshi Seeger)

anywhere. He doesn't know how to work with the establishment," Seeger later remembered the organization's vice president saying. "And to a certain extent, he was right." But then Seeger noted the lesson he learned in every campaign he waged: "The establishment never can move unless the people push 'em."[43]

Pete found that he was being pushed in the fall of 1970 by his own board of directors. One board member asked him not to sing "Waist Deep in the Big Muddy" at any *Clearwater* event. Pete could hardly believe his ears. "Look," he said, "all these subjects are tied together. You know why we don't have money to clean up this river? Guess who takes the big bite out of the tax dollar?"[44] But opposition persisted, even among those who recognized Pete and Toshi's value in raising necessary funds. When Seeger defended *Clearwater* Captain Allan Aunapu's long hair, offensive to some board members, the board considered a resolution asking him to resign. It failed by one vote. Pete saw the handwriting on the wall and gradually played a less prominent role in the organization. His dream of a sloop on the Hudson had come true. It was already drawing attention to the task of cleaning up the river. Others could take responsibility for keeping the project going.

Others did take responsibility, including lawmakers in Washington. A Water Quality Act passed in 1965 was part of President Johnson's Great Society. Amendments in 1972 established the structure for regulating the discharge of pollutants into American rivers and streams and gave the Environmental Protection Agency (EPA), established in 1970 by President Richard Nixon, authority for setting standards. What started as a labor of love created a constituency that wanted to ensure that the Hudson River, and other rivers around the nation, could be restored to a purer state.

Purity proved elusive on the Hudson. In 1975, the role of General Electric in dumping PCBs—polychlorinated biphenyls, chemicals used in the insulation of electrical equipment—into the Hudson became public. Seeger was quick to respond: "The people of America must realize we've got to organize a defense against these chemical companies."[45] The next year, the EPA banned the discharge of PCBs in rivers and other navigable waters, and eight years later, in 1984, it held GE responsible for the PCB contamination of the Hudson. Agreements in the 1990s provided for some company funding of a cleanup, but controversy—and contamination—continued to muddy the waters of the Hudson a decade later.

Even so, the Hudson River was becoming cleaner all the time. In 1986 the *New York Times* reported that people were swimming and fishing in it again. In 1994 another *Times* article noted that the river had been "brought back from the brink of disaster."[46] The *Clearwater* played an important part: it helped to spark environmental education; it spawned other boats engaged in the same tasks on the Chesapeake, on Lake Michigan, and on Long Island Sound; and it popularized the idea of river festivals around the country. Thirty-five years after its launch, at about the time of Seeger's eighty-fifth birthday, the *Clearwater* was added to the National Register of Historic Places. Seeger's dream of a boat filled with song, a boat to turn murky waters clear, was driving environmental—and social—change.

The *Clearwater* was also transforming Seeger's reputation. Some critics continued to see his environmental activism as another radical initiative, like so many of the causes he pursued. But as environmental awareness grew, Seeger's public stock, and his national role, grew as well. Folk music enthusiasts had always valued his contributions. Radicals had worked alongside him in the labor movement, the civil rights struggle, and the fight to end the war in Vietnam. But now, thanks in part to his role in imagining and constructing the *Clearwater*, others finally came to appreciate him.

A string of awards brought him added recognition in the mid-1990s. On October 14, 1994, when Seeger was seventy-five, President Bill Clinton presented him with the National Medal of the Arts, the nation's highest cultural honor. In a ceremony on the South Lawn of the White House in Washington, D.C., Clinton called the presentation to Seeger and eleven other artists "one of the great pleasures" of being president. He explained why: "It enables me to sort of relive large chunks of my life as I see the artists who have been recommended for this esteemed honor." He noted, "The arts and humanities are our bridge as a people, our bridge to one another." For Pete, the moment could only have been sweet, for Clinton was describing the very thing Seeger had sought since those early days in Harvard Yard: songs that could bring people together, span the gaps between races, between classes, between insiders and outsiders in American society.

The president singled out Seeger: "[He is someone] who had a personal impact on my life, and I would daresay, the lives of every American citizen, at least every American who is 50 years of age or younger and maybe who's 75 or 80 or younger." To drive home the point, Clinton cited "If I Had a Hammer" and "Where Have All the Flowers Gone?" and "many other songs that all of us know

Pete shaking hands with President Bill Clinton (Collection of Pete and Toshi Seeger)

by heart." The civil rights movement, the environmental movement, and the labor movement—all bore the sound of his songs: "Occasionally he still picks up his banjo, and anyone who is fortunate enough to listen will attest still to his place as one of our most enduring and endearing and important folk musicians."[47]

A month and a half later, on December 4, 1994, Seeger was one of five recipients of the Kennedy Center Honors. That ceremony, also in Washington, recognizes masters of the performing arts and is likewise one of the highlights of American cultural life. Once again, President Clinton eloquently summed up Seeger's career: "He was an inconvenient artist who dared to sing things as he saw them. He was attacked for his beliefs, he was banned from television....Some artists make musical history. Pete Seeger made history with his music."[48]

In the concert at the Kennedy Center, Arlo Guthrie sang a verse of the powerful "If I Had a Hammer," calling out Pete's grandson Tao Rodriguez to help him on another verse. Roger McGuinn, the lead singer and lead guitarist for the Byrds, sang a wonderfully melodic rendition of "Turn, Turn, Turn," a song Seeger wrote and the Byrds brought to a huge audience. Finally, Joan Baez sang the lyrical "Where Have All the Flowers Gone?"[49]

Woodcut image on the cover of Grammy-winning CD (Cover of Pete Seeger's album, *Pete,* distributed by Living Music; woodcut by Joe Servello, from photograph by Jennifer Almquist)

Other honors in this period enhanced Seeger's reputation. In 1997 he won a Grammy Award for Best Traditional Folk Album for his recording of the album *Pete* the year before. In 1999, he received the Felix Varela Medal, Cuba's highest honor, for "his humanistic and artistic work in defense of the environment and against racism." The next year, the Library of Congress named him one of America's Living Legends.[50]

In the decade that followed, Seeger continued doing the things he loved best. Though his voice showed signs of age and use he still sang and played, without charge, at local gatherings. He remained as active and enthusiastic as ever, moving from one cause to another, taking great pleasure in the issue of the moment, whether agitating against capital punishment or resisting U.S. involvement in the war in Iraq. Though "nobody really knows what the world's going to bring," he observed, and though he only felt there was "a fifty-fifty chance" of survival, he was determined to persist, saying, "As long as I've got breath, I'll keep doing what I can."[51]

And so he pushed on. He was pleased with Bruce Springsteen's CD *The Seeger Sessions* released in 2006. The internationally known rock musician recorded songs that Seeger had taught to generations of Americans and brought them back into circulation. He was likewise happy with filmmaker Jim Brown's documentary *Pete Seeger: The Power of Song*, which opened in theaters in 2007 and then aired on public television. The telephone rang incessantly, and Toshi, who still managed the mail, found herself inundated every day, as people around the country, and the world, continued to ask for his help.

The *Clearwater* remained the capstone of Seeger's career. Mobilizing thousands, it helped to set the country on a more responsible course, using the power of song to point the way to a better, cleaner America. As it rolled down the Hudson River, its soaring masts and billowing sails propelling it through the water, it underscored a powerful vision of hope and possibility and natural beauty that transcended difference. Pete expressed that vision in "My Rainbow Race," which he called "a love song for the earth":

> One blue sky above us
> One ocean lapping all our shore
> One earth so green and round
> Who could ask for more
> And because I love you
> I'll give it one more try
> To show my rainbow race
> It's too soon to die.[52]

No one could have put it better.

Afterword

∾

I FIRST SAW PETE SEEGER PERFORM IN THE SUMMER OF 1962. I was eighteen years old and preparing to start college in September. I drove with my cousin Jeff from my home in central New Jersey to visit my parents in northwestern Massachusetts, where my father was teaching at a summer workshop for high school teachers. Because they had a social commitment one evening during our stay, they got tickets for the two of us to attend a Seeger concert at the Berkshire Music Barn in nearby Lenox. Jeff, an Oberlin College banjo player, was delighted. He had seen Seeger sing folk songs many times and welcomed the chance to enjoy him again. He also told me who Pete Seeger was. I didn't know.

The evening sounded promising, even if I wasn't sure what lay ahead. I liked what little I knew about folk music. I had listened to the Kingston Trio in high school and loved songs such as "Tom Dooley" and "Sloop John B." At about the same time, my younger sister, Karen, introduced me to Peter, Paul and Mary, and their songs led me to Joan Baez and other artists who were part of the emerging folk music scene. I learned new melodies and enjoyed singing along. And I dreamed of playing the guitar myself, a desire I harbored ever since watching Elvis Presley on television years earlier.

The concert thrilled me, and I found myself joining in the choruses with everyone else. I walked out singing "Everybody Loves Saturday Night" and other songs, humming the tunes I had just heard. When I arrived at Harvard a few months later, I found some Seeger records in the music wing of Lamont Library and wandered to and from classes with "Deep Blue Sea" reverberating in my head. That summer I bought my first guitar.

I played *at* the guitar for the next thirty years. I picked up what I could from watching other people and taught myself the chords and runs I thought I needed to know. I wish I had been sensible enough to take lessons from the start, for I never got much better, but other things seemed more important at the time.

One of those things was becoming an American historian. When I finished college I went to graduate school for a year, but that first year left me uncertain about whether I actually wanted to be a historian, American or otherwise. Like many young people of my generation, I joined the Peace Corps, trying to change the world one village at a time. While stationed in Southeast Asia at the height of the war in Vietnam, I realized that what I wanted most was to study my own country. I resumed my graduate studies and soon embarked on a career of teaching and writing about the history of the twentieth-century United States. After teaching at several universities and publishing a number of books about recent American history, I began to dream about writing a biography of Seeger.

My interest in that project stemmed from my own love of music. Over the years, I would bring my guitar to class to play songs about the period we were examining. So much of what we were doing in class involved the intellect, the head, as we explored causes and consequences of this or that episode, change and continuity from one age to the next, and the all-important context of events. But I wanted more for my students. I wanted them to feel history by singing it, to touch their hearts by conjuring up the sound of the times.

For a lecture on industrialization, I played "Wabash Cannonball," a song about a railroad train that I learned from an old Seeger recording. When we studied suburbanization in the 1950s, I sang Malvina Reynolds's "Little Boxes," about the similarities of houses in suburbia, a song Seeger popularized. For the civil rights movement, naturally, I played "We Shall Overcome." In that lecture, I put the words up on the PowerPoint screen and asked my 360 students to cross their arms, join hands, and sing along with me, just as students had in the 1960s. I knew the exercise was hokey, and the students laughed sheepishly at first, but I felt just like Pete Seeger as I cajoled them into singing out. Soon they were swaying back and forth to the rhythm of the song.

The idea of a biography of Seeger intrigued me. However many of his songs I could sing, I didn't know all the contours of his life. I knew he had been part of the Weavers, and I had listened to many of his recordings of the old American folk songs that he was trying to revive. To me, the project seemed like a good fit. But when I started to read in depth in the early 1990s, I came across David Dunaway's book *How Can I Keep from Singing: Pete Seeger*, published a decade before, and figured that his work preempted any effort of my own. Reluctantly, I moved on.

About ten years later, I had a stroke of good luck. While conducting research at the Franklin D. Roosevelt Library in Hyde Park I had dinner with an old friend from graduate school and one of the editors of a newly launched series stressing the role of narrative in writing about American history. We talked about storytelling and about music, for both of his children were accomplished fiddle players. I told him about my interest in performing, and finally taking lessons to make such appearances possible. He mentioned his hope of having one of the series volumes deal with a musical theme. Pete Seeger immediately came to mind. His life cut across the twentieth century and hit upon issues that had always intrigued me: the union movement of the 1930s and 1940s, the anti-Communist crusade of the 1950s, the struggle for civil rights of the 1950s and 1960s, the war in Vietnam in the 1960s, and the environmental activism of the 1970s and the decades that followed. By the time dinner was over, I was ready to put together a proposal, David Dunaway's book notwithstanding.

As I began work on my book, I recognized that this project posed its own problems. There was no collection of Seeger papers in any library or archive. I had access to newspaper and magazine articles, published interviews, old copies of *Sing Out!*, song lyrics and recordings on old vinyl records and new CDs, all of which would be essential in my work. In addition, Seeger himself had put together two useful collections of his musings about music and its role in public life. Both *The Incompleat Folksinger*, edited by Jo Metcalf Schwartz and published in 1972, and *Where Have All the Flowers Gone: A Singer's Stories, Songs, Seeds, Robberies*, published in 1993, provided a good starting point. As I delved into those materials, I returned to David Dunaway's book and found that it gave me the context and framework I needed. When I went to Washington, D.C., in the spring of 2007 to attend a symposium celebrating the entire Seeger family, I learned that Dunaway had deposited in the Library of Congress's American Folklife Center transcripts of interviews with Seeger, and those proved helpful, too. The best footage of Seeger singing I found was in Jim Brown's powerful documentary film *Pete Seeger: The Power of Song,* which appeared just as I was completing a first draft.[1]

But Seeger, in his late eighties, was still very much alive, and I wanted to talk to him myself. A vast collection of published interviews gave me important insights into the high points of his career, but I had to meet him, to ask my own questions, and to try to understand how he now viewed his musical and political activities over the past seventy years.

Tracking him down was a problem. I knew that he lived along the Hudson River and learned that his home was in Beacon, about an hour north of New York City, but I could find neither an address nor a phone number. Knowing of his work with the sloop *Clearwater,* I contacted officers of the organization that handled the boat and wrote a few letters to be forwarded to Seeger, but to no avail. Then a web search revealed a contact for the agent of his half-sister, Peggy, also a singer and songwriter. When I spoke to the agent and explained what I was doing, he was willing to contact the Seegers and leave them my phone number in the hope that Pete would call. A week or so later he did, and we began a series of conversations that ended up with my making the first of many trips to Beacon in August 2006.

Pete met me at the train station and drove me up the hill to his house overlooking the Hudson. Nervously, I set up the tape recorder, and we spoke about his family, his background, and his involvement in all the areas I planned to cover. When I turned off the tape recorder three and a half hours later, Pete made lunch for us out of leftovers Toshi had in the refrigerator. After eating, I said, "Pete, I'd like to ask you a favor."

"What's that?" he asked.

"Would you play that thing for me?" I said, pointing to his long-necked banjo, hanging on the living room wall. It contained the inscription "THIS MACHINE SURROUNDS HATE AND FORCES IT TO SURRENDER" in capital letters in a circle around the perimeter of the flat banjo belly.

Pete with his banjo (and its inscription) (Collection of Pete and Toshi Seeger)

"Only if you'll play with me," he said, looking at my guitar, which I had sheepishly laid in the center of the room. That response, of course, was precisely what I had hoped to hear.

After tuning up, we played songs I chose. We did "Oh, Mary, Don't You Weep," one of his favorite old gospel hymns, "We Shall Overcome," "Goodnight, Irene," and Woody Guthrie's great "This Land Is Your Land." On a couple of them, we made it all the way through, and then he said, "I really prefer to do this one more slowly," and so we did it again. Finally I thanked him, and we put our instruments down.

Later I came across a comment by his grandson Tao Rodriguez, an avid musician himself, after he performed with Seeger at a river festival. Speaking first about his own volunteer work, he added, "But for me, the ultimate is just to play with Grandpa."[2] I felt the same way.

Other trips to Beacon followed. In December, Seeger told me that he was planning to have a monthly series of songfests in the village, each on a Saturday night when local merchants stayed open late for the holiday season. I decided I wanted to see him do what he had been doing so well for so many years—getting people to sing—and I returned to the Hudson River Valley for the holidays. This time, Pete spoke on tape again for a while and made copies for me of some of his own materials dealing with his work in the 1940s for *People's Songs*. We went downtown and rigged up a makeshift sound system, drawing current from the battery in his pickup truck. In the bone-chilling evening, he started playing and we all joined in. Others soon took the lead and chose what they wanted to sing. Pete played along in the background, clearly satisfied with the result. Watching him surrounded by a hundred friends and neighbors who ignored the cold, brought their own instruments, and sang together, I sensed the power in his song.

I returned a year later to fill in some gaps in what I had written. As one visit followed another, I grew more comfortable. This trip was the best yet. Over a breakfast of buckwheat pancakes Toshi made, the three of us chatted in the kitchen about politics and current affairs, then Pete lit a fire in the living room and we talked for a couple of hours on tape. When I had what I needed, I switched off the recorder and again, much less self-consciously, asked him to play some music with me. "Of course," he said, taking a smaller banjo off the wall. This time he began by picking out the tune of Woody Guthrie's "Reuben James," and I was able to follow with my version of "Wildwood Flower," set to the same tune. I started to play "My Get Up and Go," his song about getting old, and he immediately joined in, singing loudest of all on the choruses. When a small visitor, the son of friends who were visiting, wandered into the living room, together we played Guthrie's "Mail Myself to You," a song I played for my own daughter when she was three or four.

As we played together, I realized that as much as he was a performer, Pete also saw himself as a teacher, eager to engage people in doing what he loved best. As he once put it, "A great many members of my family have been teachers, and so am I, after a fashion."[3] His mission had been to get Americans, and people around the world, singing songs. Once, while he was still middle aged, he paused for a moment as he finished singing "Deep Blue Sea" and reflected on the early gatherings of the Almanac Singers, when people got together for the sheer enjoyment of singing songs. Those days seemed long ago, he said. "Now I begin to feel like old Grandpa. But I'm proudest of all that I've been able to be a kind of a link in a chain for a lot of people to learn some good songs."[4]

Much later, as he looked back on his experiences with the *Clearwater*, he amplified on that idea. "I'm a great believer in the old biblical story of the sower of seeds," he observed. "A sower scatters seeds, and some fall on stones. They don't even sprout. Some fall in the pathway; they sprout but they get stamped on. But some seeds fall on fallow ground and grow and multiply a thousandfold. And I look upon myself as a sower of seeds, all my life."[5]

As I thought about my own experience of playing a few songs with him, I realized that I had become another member of a still-growing contingent of followers to whom he could pass on his belief in the power of song. Though I wondered if he would be willing to play with me, I finally understood that this was what he always wanted. Not only did I appreciate the sheer pleasure of playing with him, but I also valued the sense of being one more link in his long musical chain.

My interviews with Seeger proved useful. Each time I returned home, I had the tape recordings transcribed and read through our conversations, attentive both to what Seeger said and to what the exchange revealed about how he viewed his life and career. But as I went over transcriptions, I realized that much of what he told me echoed what he told others in countless published and unpublished interviews and what he wrote in his own essays and books. He clearly thought about the role of music in his life, and in our collective life, and knew how he wanted to frame his observations for anyone who would listen. It was not a question of staying on script, as a politician often must do, but rather of having come to a sense of what he wanted to share with interviewers over the years. If anything, the similarities in his statements underscored the continuities in his life and persuaded me that I was on the right track as I tried to pull my story together.

The narrative proved to be a different kind of challenge. I had always sought to write readable prose, accessible to general audiences, but that was different from trying to sustain a story true to the energy and activity of Seeger's life. Some years ago, I had tried my hand at fiction and written a children's novel, *Cassie's War*, about a young girl's experience during World War II. With the assistance of a good friend and accomplished novelist, I came to understand how to plot a scene, how to highlight detail to create a sense of immediacy, how to use dialogue to carry the story along. But in the process I also discovered how difficult it was to let the characters tell the story rather than telling it myself. I wanted so strongly to describe the impact of the wartime home front that I fear I battered readers with what I thought they needed to know, rather than letting such an awareness unfold in the course of telling the story.

In writing narrative history, dialogue was different from writing fiction. Working on the novel, I found myself listening to voices in my mind as I tried to capture the emotional reality of what was being said. In this book, I had to listen to what Seeger and others said to find details I needed to make the story come alive and then weave them all together.

I also found myself reflecting about dramatic flow. In fiction, action often points to a climax at the end of the piece. As I worked through the various episodes of Seeger's life, it seemed to me that his confrontation with HUAC in the 1950s, with his willingness to go to jail in defense of his political beliefs in the 1960s, was a climactic event. It certainly seemed to me the most dramatic incident in his life. The only problem was that it came midway through my story. Yet given the configurations of Seeger's career, there was no way that I could save that episode for last.

Still another question emerged as I completed an early draft. How could I deal respectfully with a biographical subject who was very much alive and still ensure that the overall assessment remained my own? I admired Seeger, even more so as I became intensely familiar with everything he had done in his life. He had his foibles, as we all do, but still made some remarkable contributions to American musical life and political culture. I wanted to recognize those accomplishments, but in my own way and with my own sense of historical context.

Dunaway confronted the same question decades earlier. In a revised edition of *How Can I Keep from Singing* published in 1990, he described his association with Seeger. "When I began this book in 1975," he wrote, "Seeger agreed to help but from the first cautioned me that this would not be an authorized biography, nor would he read the manuscript in draft form." Dunaway quoted Seeger as saying, "I've turned down all biographers. I really feel there are other people worth writing about, and I've had too much publicity already."

Dunaway's biography appeared in 1981 and won the Deems Taylor Award from the American Society of Composers, Authors, and Publishers. People interested in folk music and the folk revival regard it as a necessary starting point. Seeger read the book carefully and suggested several corrections, ranging, in Dunaway's words, "from photo captions to the number of times his eldest brother was married to adding new lyrics for a favorite song."[6] Dunaway incorporated the suggestions into a revised edition, which Seeger also read with equal attentiveness in the summer of 1999. During one of my visits, Pete shared with me his copy of the latest paperback edition, with scores of his comments scribbled in red ink in the margins. On the title page, he noted that he had gone over the entire text with Dunaway the following summer and included even more suggestions, this time in black ink.[7]

Seeger also raised another issue about Dunaway's work. He told me, in the course of casual conversation, that he sometimes thought Dunaway tried too hard to intuit what he was feeling, and certain assessments about his reactions to particular incidents or events made him uncomfortable. That critique, of course, got at the heart of the dilemma of writing about a living subject and made me conscious of the need for care in framing my own conclusions. It also helped me become exquisitely aware of the need to make careful choices about what to accept and what to reject of Seeger's reactions to ensure that the argument in my book remained my own.

I found out for myself just how attentive Seeger was to detail when I first wrote to him. I sent along the book proposal I had drafted for my publisher, along with an early version of the prologue. When he finally responded, he included his comments and annotations for my benefit. Though he joked about how his memory was deteriorating and complained about not being able to remember what he had for breakfast that morning, he had an uncanny recollection of how events in his life had unfolded four and five decades before.

Over the next year and a half, I shared more of my own material with Seeger. He read and critiqued a short essay I wrote and appeared comfortable with my focus. I also wanted him to see the entire text, and we finally agreed that we would go through it together. In May 2008, I spent two enormously useful days with Pete and Toshi. We went over every page; it took more than twelve hours. As Pete corrected chronology and pointed out occasional errors, I made the changes myself. Occasionally he or Toshi raised questions about a word or a phrase, and we talked about possible alternatives. I took pleasure watching him chuckle from time to time and left relieved that both he and Toshi liked what I had done.

Beyond all the caveats and concerns about writing about a living subject, other fundamental questions remained. What was the source of Seeger's appeal? How did he manage to capture the attention and affection of people around the world? And why is song such a powerful medium? As I moved forward with my project, I found myself coming back to that first concert I saw at the Music Barn in the summer of 1962. Seeger was, quite simply, a masterful performer.

Then and in every other performance I saw in person or on film, I realized that above all Seeger understood his audience. He always appeared calm and casual, but in fact he had thought out ahead of time just where he wanted a concert to go and how he hoped listeners would react. "I like to start off a program with a song that is mostly instrumental on banjo or guitar," he once observed. "Why? I guess because the music says more about who I am and what I want to do than a whole string of words."[8] But he also had the power to exhort. At a civil rights concert at Carnegie Hall in New York City in the spring of 1963, just before he and his family began their world tour, he told his audience, "If you want to get out of a pessimistic mood yourself, I've got one *sure* remedy. Go help those people in Birmingham or Mississippi." And as he drifted into "Oh, Freedom," the crowd roared.[9]

Seeger described this pattern as he prepared to perform in Meridian, Mississippi, in the summer of 1964. "My program was essentially not too different from what I always give," he recalled soon after. "A few old songs, hinting at the history of our country. A few songs from other countries, hinting at the different types of people in this big world—but also good songs which will give us a feeling of friendship to them. A few stories or songs for kids, such as 'Abiyoyo,' the allegory on the power of music. But my audience was happiest when, near the end, I concentrated on what they call 'our' songs, the spirituals and gospel songs with freedom verses which have swept through the South in the last few years."[10]

Seeger recognized that songs could describe the resonance of relationships. Repeated refrains helped create a harmonious mood. The perennial favorite "Abiyoyo" told how music was responsible for the demise of a wicked giant, making the world safer for all. With a banjo accompaniment, it tells the story of a small boy who plays the ukulele and his magician father who makes things disappear. After townspeople tire of the noise and tricks and banish the boy and his father, they find themselves oppressed by Abiyoyo, a terrible giant who terrorizes the town. But the boy makes the giant dance himself into exhaustion, and his father makes the giant disappear, to everyone's delight.[11]

Seeger also knew how songs complemented one another. He once observed that he often sang the gentle and melodic song "The Water Is Wide" after raising the roof with "If I Had a Hammer." In making the transition he told audiences, "All our militance, enthusiasm, bravery will count for nothing if we can't cross the oceans of misunderstanding between the peoples of this world."[12]

At the heart of the power of Seeger's songs lay the participation of the audience. He had an uncanny knack of getting people to sing along. "The revival of audience singing is an integral part of the whole revival of interest in folk songs," he said in 1956. "Consider the matter historically. It is only within recent human history that such emphasis has been put upon professional solo singers. In primitive tribes all songs, except for the long narratives, were sung by everyone. If a song had a chorus, everybody in the audience naturally sang it."[13] Singing together created a sense of social cohesion. It involved people in a shared activity. It could foster a common understanding. As he observed, "Singing together, you suddenly find out there's things that you can learn from each other that you wouldn't learn with arguments and which you might not learn any other way."[14]

Seeger thought carefully about how to get people to sing. It was not easy at the start. "When I first started singing folk songs," he recalled, "it was like pulling teeth to get anyone to sing with me." He learned to explain what he wanted an audience to do, but he also knew that "too much talking is the death of music." He discovered how "to loosen an audience up and make them lose self-consciousness. A good belly laugh is one of the best ways to do this, but don't risk the sour aftertaste of an unsuccessful attempt at humor." There was one final element: the right musical key, one that everybody could sing, with care given to rhythm and pacing to ensure that songs ran longer rather than shorter, so the involvement of the audience could grow with each stanza.[15]

Arlo Guthrie, Woody's son, captured Seeger's technique in a concert they did together in the summer of 1981. Guthrie was about to teach the audience to sing the "Garden Song," which he often performed. "I've been watching Pete now for a few years," he told the audience, "and he does something I can't do, which is he sings the song twice at the same time. He sings the song once in front of the song and then once with everybody. That's hard."[16] But it worked.

Others shared Guthrie's admiration. "Pete makes it all look easy," according to the folksinger Michael Cooney. "Don't believe it. All great art looks simple, but Pete's professional reputation was built on musicianship. His appearance of ease is deliberate. 'Look at me,' he seems to say, 'I don't have a voice as smooth as dewdrops rolling off rose petals—you can sing this too.'"[17] Seeger's half-sister, Peggy, was equally impressed. "It's amazing how Pete does it," she said. "He's perfected certain motions and things you say to an audience until it seems spontaneous. He'll pick out one person in the crowd and address something to them. This helps the singer look on the audience as an aggregate of individuals, rather than a blurry mass."[18]

Seeger understood his own special bond with an audience. As he wrote in his "Johnny Appleseed, Jr." column in *Sing Out!* in 1960, "As a performer, yours truly does not have much of a voice, and there are plenty of young people who can play rings around me on guitar or banjo. But I'm proud that I've hardly ever met an audience I couldn't get singing. I figure my main function in life is that of a sort of catalyst, bringing some good people together with some good songs."[19] Seeger recognized his ability to perform a kind of musical alchemy that transformed a passive audience into an active force. Everything pointed to creating a community of singers. And such a community could become an instrument of social change.

With a strong sense of self-awareness, Seeger was always quick to acknowledge important influences in his life. "I think Woody was the biggest single influence," he once observed. "And then black musicians I knew, like Lead Belly and Brownie McGee and Bernice Reagon. I've perhaps learned more from them than I could ever describe because they got me to loosen up. I tend to be a little tight, like most New Englanders. . . . I think I've learned a little bit about relaxing from the African-American musicians I know."[20]

Seeger's style made him a folk music icon. "All he has to do, for me," the folksinger Tom Paxton once observed, "is stand up there, and hit that instrument, tell us what the song is, and play along with us," and a concert or gathering was successful.[21] I saw that firsthand when I attended a concert at the Library of Congress in the winter of 2007. Pete, Peggy, and his half-brother, Mike, simply walked onstage and the audience rose almost as one, applauding wildly for nearly five minutes. The way Seeger conducted himself conveyed a fundamental decency and integrity. He believed passionately in the causes he sang about, and his actions demonstrated that he was prepared to make good on his commitments. "I really love this country," he observed. "If you love your country, you'll find ways somehow to speak out to do what you think is right."[22] After years with the Weavers, he left the group when the others wanted to record a lucrative cigarette commercial. In the dark days of the second Red Scare, he was prepared to go to jail in defense of his First Amendment rights.

There was a consistency to the positions he took throughout his life, which enabled him to move from one cause to another with a sense of enthusiasm and optimism. He was, as the author and journalist Studs Terkel described him, "the boy with that touch of hope in the midst of bleakness."[23] He understood that social and political change took time, that progress came step by small step, that the failures of one era could someday lead to success, that the battle required constant exertion. As he remarked in mid-1965, "History shows that there is a hidden heritage of militancy which comes and goes, but never completely dies. It undergoes transformations and permutations from century to century, but the lessons learned by one generation, even though in defeat, are passed on to the next."[24] He was willing to face turbulence and was fond of quoting the nineteenth-century black activist Frederick Douglass, who once said, "Those who would like to see progress without a struggle are those who would like to see Niagara without the roar of the waters."[25]

To those who questioned his involvement with the Communist Party he acknowledged "not seeing that Stalin was a supremely cruel misleader." Occasionally naïve in pursuit of a cause, Seeger was still nobody's fool. In 1995, he wryly observed, "I still call myself a communist, because communism is no more what Russia made of it than Christianity is what the churches make of it."[26]

Personal integrity reflected political integrity. Though Woody Guthrie sometimes griped affectionately about Seeger's puritanical personal habits and joked about his difficulty understanding someone who didn't smoke, drink, or chase women, he respected his friend's positions. Seeger himself observed that Toshi's running joke was "If only Peter would chase women instead of chasing causes, I'd have an excuse to leave him."[27] And he was fond of telling a story that was in fact a personal parable. There was, he said, a tiny peace demonstration in Times Square in the 1950s. An onlooker scoffed at a Quaker carrying a sign, saying, "Do you think you're going to change the world by standing here at midnight with that sign?"

"I suppose not," the young man said, "but I'm going to make sure the world doesn't change me."[28]

Seeger never completed college, but he was comfortable with the world of ideas and read widely on his own. While he avoided references from his reading while performing, he sprinkled his casual conversation with quotations from Plato, Aristotle, and a host of other philosophers, but always in a way that avoided seeming pedantic or pretentious. He had simply come across an idea that intrigued him and wanted to share it with anyone who would listen.

Though he came from a family of some sophistication, he never ceased portraying himself as a common man. His dress was always casual: jeans, sometimes overalls, and work shirts. He was proud of having built his log cabin entirely by his own hand. He was fond of telling stories and loved to talk about his travels with Woody, sometimes at his own expense, laughing as he confessed that the first train he jumped never managed to leave the freight

Pete relaxing with his banjo (Collection of Pete and Toshi Seeger)

yard. All of that reflected an attitude that fellow Weaver Lee Hays affectionately called "arrogant modesty." But it remained at the root of his appeal.[29]

As his reputation grew and he became a household name, at least in some circles, he depended on Toshi, without always acknowledging her important contributions. In the early years, particularly as he took off to perform at camps and colleges, she made all the arrangements; she handled the contracts and finances and ensured that he could concentrate on doing what he did best. In time, he had managers, but for a while, it was Toshi who managed almost everything. Pete later observed that he was often too busy to be a good father. "Half the time I was away singing some place," he said. "One year Toshi counted the days I was home: 90 out of the year's 365."[30] She herself observed, "[The] complete isolation wasn't good for me or the children in the long run."[31] As always, she gave up things important to her with a shrug: "I just do what I have to do."[32]

Years later, Pete still regretted asking Toshi to leave the young children with her parents to join him when the Weavers were performing for several months on the West Coast. He spoke appreciatively about "her patience" with him as the key to a long and successful relationship.[33] He described "a cartoon on the wall of my office showing a harried woman with a kid pulling at her skirt and she's on the phone: 'No, he's not here. He's out trying to save oppressed people.'"[34] Toshi, in the words of Seeger's brother John, "enabled Pete to be Pete."[35] But she always remained in the background, and audiences saw only Seeger, with his charismatic presence, on center stage. Even when I asked a question that involved them both, Pete answered. Toshi joked about it, knowing she was perfectly capable of speaking for herself. Pete just smiled, as Toshi took over the narrative. When she finished, he proceeded from the point he had left off.

In concerts, personal appearances, and assorted writings, Seeger conveyed his passionate sense that music made a difference. When I pressed him to explain what communism meant to him, why he joined the Party and stayed with it for a time, I realized how much he saw music as the frame to the world around him. Music was where it began for him. The labor arts movement that drew young, talented idealists to radical causes was his point of entry. Not that he didn't believe in his many causes. But what held them all together was the music, and the commitment to bringing people together through it. He believed that songs "can help this world survive." He was realistic about how much songs could accomplish: "Songs won't save the planet. But, then, neither will books or speeches....Songs are sneaky things. They can slip across borders. Proliferate in prisons. Penetrate hard shells." He was—and is—fond of quoting Plato: "Rulers should be careful about what songs are allowed to be sung."[36] Singer Bruce Springsteen summed up Seeger's passion: "Pete was one of those guys that saw himself as citizen artist, as activist. He had a very full idea about those things, how it connected to music and what music could do. The power that music had, to influence, to inspire. And that's the power of folk music, and that's the power of Pete Seeger."[37]

Seeger shared that sense of the importance of singing with audiences throughout his life. In the 1930s and early 1940s, he believed that music could help the labor movement achieve its ends. He dreamed of masses of workers singing such classics as "Solidarity Forever" along with the songs that he and Guthrie and others wrote. "I've seen a bunch of strikers being given courage by union songs," he once observed.[38] When labor activism lost steam, he sang about the dangers of the nuclear age and the need to speak out against oppression, whether domestic or foreign. During the civil rights era of the 1960s, he helped to turn "We Shall Overcome" into the anthem of the movement for black equality. Furious at the continuing involvement of the United States in Vietnam, he honestly, if a bit innocently, believed that if he could sing antiwar songs on television he could bring Americans to their senses. He had the best chance to achieve his dream when he took the lead in helping build the *Clearwater,* complete with a crew of folksingers who traveled up and down the Hudson River, trying to persuade both politicians and the people to support the cause.

Seeger's appeal rested not just on how he appeared in performance but on the songs he wrote. Less prolific than Woody Guthrie, who could turn out a song a day, Seeger has left us songs that have become standards of the folk music canon. With its driving rhythms, "If I Had a Hammer" still captures the need to stand up to injustice and support the cause of liberty. "Where Have all the Flowers Gone?" is a plaintive, lyrical appeal to stop the cycle of war. "We Shall Overcome" is sung all over the world whenever there is a struggle for freedom.

Other songs continue to resonate in the same way. "Guantanamera," which Seeger popularized, uses verses from a poem by the late nineteenth-century Cuban freedom fighter José Martí, set to an old Cuban melody. Seeger also brought other songs from around the world to America. One of the best-known and most widely sung is "Wimoweh." Originally recorded in 1939 by Solomon Linda, a black South African, as "Mbube," Zulu for "The Lion," it is a simple song that became enormously popular in his own country. When Seeger heard it he misinterpreted the word *mbube* as "wimoweh," which is how the Weavers recorded it and made it part of their repertoire.

In 1959, as the Red Scare faded, Seeger wrote a song that unwittingly served as a précis for all he had done and all he would do. It came in response to a request from his publisher for something other than the same old protest songs he was turning out. Irritated at the request and perhaps still smarting from the ordeal of the Red Scare, Seeger fired back, "You better find another songwriter. This is the only kind of song I know how to write." Still, the appeal got him thinking. He looked at the pocket notebook in which he jotted down ideas, lyrics, snippets of prose that intrigued him, anything that might find its way into a song. He came across some verses from the Book of Ecclesiastes he had copied a year earlier. He omitted a few lines, repeated a couple of others, and threw in one of his own at the end. He also added one other word, repeated three times, in the chorus. After figuring out a melody, he sent it off to his publisher, who was enthusiastic.

"Turn, Turn, Turn" became a huge hit when it was recorded by the rock group the Byrds in 1965. Seeger liked that version, "all those electric guitars. Like clanging bells." When I asked him for help in playing the song in the late fall of 2007, he told me that he appreciated the way the group changed the melody slightly in the last line of each verse, and because most people knew their rendition, that was how he sang it now.[39]

For Seeger, the song summed up his own life. He fought for justice, in one form or another, time after time. Each time, he did everything he could, and when he could do no more, or when the ground shifted under him, he found another cause, each one accompanied by a song of the times and all of them songs for the ages. As the biblical verse and the song both say, "To everything there is a season, and a time for every purpose under heaven." So it was for Seeger, a season for every cause and a purpose for every time.

Notes

Prologue

1. David Dunaway, *How Can I Keep from Singing: Pete Seeger* (New York: Da Capo Press, 1990), 52.

2. Ibid., 39.

3. Allan M. Winkler interview with Pete Seeger, Beacon, New York, August 3, 2006.

4. Ibid.

5. Dunaway, *How Can I Keep from Singing,* 39.

6. Ibid.

7. David Dunaway interview with Pete Seeger, July 19, 1976, David Dunaway/Pete Seeger Interviews Collection, AFC 2000/019, Box 1, Folder 6, American Folklife Center, Library of Congress.

8. Winkler interview with Pete Seeger, August 3, 2006.

9. Dunaway, *How Can I Keep from Singing,* 43.

10. Ibid., 49.

11. David Dunaway interview with Pete Seeger, March 9, 1977, David Dunaway/Pete Seeger Interviews Collection, Box 1, Folder 10.

12. Dunaway, *How Can I Keep from Singing,* 51.

13. Winkler interview with Pete Seeger, August 3, 2006.

14. Dunaway, *How Can I Keep from Singing,* 53.

ONE

1. Allan M. Winkler interview with Pete Seeger, August 3, 2006.

2. Conversation quoted in David Dunaway, *How Can I Keep from Singing: Pete Seeger* (New York: Da Capo Press, 1990), 59.

3. Winkler interview with Pete Seeger, August 3, 2006.

4. Ibid.

5. Pete Seeger, *The Incompleat Folksinger*, edited by Jo Metcalf Schwartz (New York: Simon & Schuster, 1972), 12.

6. Seeger quoted in Dunaway, *How Can I Keep from Singing*, 58.

7. Seeger, *Incompleat Folksinger*, 28.

8. Ibid., 34.

9. Allan M. Winkler interview with Pete and Toshi Seeger, Beacon, New York, April 18, 2008; see also Pete Seeger, *Where Have All the Flowers Gone: A Singer's Stories, Songs, Seeds, Robberies* (Bethlehem, Penn.: Sing Out Corporation, 1993), 17.

10. Seeger, *Where Have All the Flowers Gone*, 17.

11. Ibid.; Winkler interview with Pete Seeger, August 3, 2006.

12. Lomax quoted in Dunaway, *How Can I Keep from Singing*, 61.

13. Seeger quoted in Dunaway, *How Can I Keep from Singing*, 61.

14. David Dunaway interview with Pete Seeger, March 9, 1977, Box 1, Folder 10, David Dunaway/Pete Seeger Interviews Collection, Library of Congress.

15. Pete Seeger, quoted in the television documentary *Woody Guthrie: Ain't Got No Home*, written, produced, and directed by Peter Frumkin (PBS, 2006).

16. Seeger, *Incompleat Folksinger*, 42–43.

17. Seeger quoted in documentary *Woody Guthrie*.

18. Lomax quoted in Dunaway, *How Can I Keep from Singing*, 64.

19. Seeger, *Incompleat Folksinger*, 43.

20. Guthrie quoted in Dunaway, *How Can I Keep from Singing*, 65.

21. Guthrie quoted in David Dunaway interview with Pete Seeger, April 15, 1976, Box 1, Folder 5, David Dunaway/Pete Seeger Interviews Collection.

22. Winkler interview with Pete Seeger, August 3, 2006.

23. Scott Simon, "Interview: Folk Singer Pete Seeger Talks about His Career Writing and Singing Folk Music," *Weekend Edition,* National Public Radio, July 2, 2005.

24. Seeger, *Incompleat Folksinger,* 14.

25. Winkler interview with Pete Seeger, August 3, 2006.

26. Seeger, *Incompleat Folksinger,* 58.

27. Introduction to "66 Highway Blues," in *Hard Hitting Songs for Hard-Hit People,* compiled by Alan Lomax, notes on the songs by Woody Guthrie, music transcribed and edited by Pete Seeger (New York: Oak Publications, 1967), 62.

28. *Hard Hitting Songs,* 62–63. Pete Seeger, Woody Guthrie © 1966 (Renewed), Stormking Music, Inc. 50% All rights reserved. Used by permission.

29. One version of this song appears in *Hard Hitting Songs,* 324–325.

30. Introduction to "Union Maid" in *Hard Hitting Songs,* 324.

31. Timothy P. Lynch, *Strike Songs of the Depression* (Jackson: University Press of Mississippi, 2001), 124–125.

32. Joe Klein, *Woody Guthrie: A Life* (New York: Ballantine Books, 1980), 188.

33. Hays quoted in Dunaway, *How Can I Keep from Singing,* 76.

34. Seeger, *Incompleat Folksinger,* 15.

35. Winkler interview with Pete and Toshi Seeger, April 18, 2008.

36. *Daily Worker* story quoted in Klein, *Woody Guthrie,* 192.

37. Dreiser quoted in Klein, *Woody Guthrie,* 192.

38. Seeger, *Where Have All the Flowers Gone,* 21. Lee Hays, Millard Lampell © 1993, Stormking Music, Inc. All rights reserved. Used by permission.

39. "June Records," *Time,* June 16, 1941, 60.

40. "The Poison in Our System," *Atlantic Monthly,* June 1941, 661.

41. Eleanor Roosevelt quoted in Klein, *Woody Guthrie,* 197; Franklin D. Roosevelt quoted in Seeger, *Where Have All the Flowers Gone,* 22.

42. Winkler interview with Pete Seeger, August 3, 2006.

43. "Talking Union" in Seeger, *Where Have All the Flowers Gone,* 23. Lee Hays, Millard Lampell, Pete Seeger © 1946, Stormking Music, Inc. All rights reserved. Used by permission.

44. Seeger, *Incompleat Folksinger,* 15.

45. Ibid., 16.

46. Seeger, *Where Have All the Flowers Gone,* 27.

47. *World-Telegram* story quoted in Dunaway, *How Can I Keep from Singing,* 102.

48. Winkler interview with Pete Seeger, August 3, 2006.

49. Ibid.

50. Dunaway, *How Can I Keep from Singing,* 108.

51. Winkler interview with Pete Seeger, August 3, 2006.

52. *Sing Out!* August/September 1966, 61.

53. Seeger quoted in Dunaway, *How Can I Keep from Singing,* 114.

54. Ibid., 116.

55. Seeger, *Where Have All the Flowers Gone,* 16.

56. Seeger, *Incompleat Folksinger,* 568.

Two

1. Mario (Boots) Cassetta, quoted in David Dunaway, *How Can I Keep from Singing: Pete Seeger* (New York: Da Capo Press, 1990), 112.

2. Ibid., 117.

3. Ibid.

4. Pete Seeger, "Foreword," in *Reprints from the People's Songs Bulletin* (New York: Oak Publications, Inc., 1961), 3.

5. Ibid.

6. Pete Seeger, *The Incompleat Folksinger,* edited by Jo Metcalf Schwartz (New York: Simon & Schuster, 1972), 20.

7. Facsimile of vol. 1, no. 1, in *Reprints from the People's Songs Bulletin,* 6.

8. *Reprints from the People's Songs Bulletin.*

9. Lee Hays, "A Sermon to Songwriters," in *"Sing Out, Warning! Sing Out, Love!": The Writings of Lee Hays,* edited by Robert S. Koppelman (Amherst: University of Massachusetts Press, 2003), 89.

10. Seeger, *Incompleat Folksinger,* 327.

11. "Hootenanny," *Time,* April 15, 1946, 72.

12. Woody Guthrie quoted in Ronald D. Cohen, *Rainbow Quest: The Folk Music Revival and American Society, 1940–1970* (Amherst: University of Massachusetts Press, 2002), 43.

13. Seeger, *Incompleat Folksinger,* 328.

14. Edwin E. Gordon, "Cultivating Songs of the People," *New York Times,* August 25, 1946.

15. Allan M. Winkler interview with Pete and Toshi Seeger, Beacon, New York, April 18, 2008.

16. Michael Gold quoted in Cohen, *Rainbow Quest,* 42.

17. *Congressional Record,* 79th Congress, 2nd session (vol. 92, part 9, Appendix), A1146.

18. Cohen, *Rainbow Quest,* 44.

19. *Broadcasting* quoted in Cohen, *Rainbow Quest,* 46.

20. Woltman quoted in Cohen, *Rainbow Quest,* 46.

21. Report quoted in Cohen, *Rainbow Quest,* 46.

22. Seeger quoted in Cohen, *Rainbow Quest,* 120.

23. *Billboard* and *New Yorker* quoted in Cohen, *Rainbow Quest,* 23.

24. Silber quoted in Cohen, *Rainbow Quest,* 55.

25. FBI informant quoted in Dunaway, *How Can I Keep from Singing,* 125.

26. Seeger quoted in Dunaway, *How Can I Keep from Singing,* 127.

27. Pete Seeger typed reflections on People's Songs, provided during interview, December 9, 2006.

28. Seeger, "Foreword," 3.

29. Allan M. Winkler telephone interview with Pete Seeger, October 4, 2006.

30. Seeger quoted in Dunaway, *How Can I Keep from Singing,* 133.

31. David Dunaway interview with Pete Seeger, March 6, 1977, Box 1, Folder 9, David Dunaway/Pete Seeger Interviews Collection, Library of Congress.

32. Seeger quoted in Dunaway, *How Can I Keep from Singing,* 134.

33. David Dunaway interview with Pete Seeger, March 6, 1977, Box 1, Folder 9, David Dunaway/Pete Seeger Interviews Collection.

34. Winkler interview with Pete and Toshi Seeger, April 18, 2008.

35. Ibid. See also John W. Whitehead, "When Will They Ever Learn? An Interview with Pete Seeger," *OldSpeak,* January 4, 2006, at http://www.rutherford.org/Oldspeak/Articles/Art/oldspeak-Seeger.html.

36. Silber quoted in Cohen, *Rainbow Quest,* 62–63.

37. Seeger, *Incompleat Folksinger,* 464.

38. Cohen, *Rainbow Quest,* 63.

39. Seeger, *Incompleat Folksinger,* 465.

40. Ibid.

41. Howard Fast, *Peekskill USA: Inside the Infamous 1949 Riots* (1951; Mineola, N.Y.: Dover, 2006), 87.

42. Hays quoted in Cohen, *Rainbow Quest,* 63.

43. Robert Cantwell, *When We Were Good: The Folk Revival* (Cambridge, Mass.: Harvard University Press, 1996), 178.

44. Scott Simon, "Interview: Folk Singer Pete Seeger Talks about His Career Writing and Singing Folk Music," *Weekend Edition,* National Public Radio, July 2, 2005.

45. "The Hammer Song," in *Sing Out!* vol.1, no. 1 (May 1950): cover. See Pete Seeger, *Where Have All the Flowers Gone: A Singer's Stories, Songs, Seeds, Robberies* (Bethlehem, Penn.: Sing Out Corporation, 1993), 40–41, for the later Peter, Paul, and Mary version.

46. Robert S. Koppelman, "Introduction: Lee Hays, American Culture, and the American Left," in Hays, *"Sing Out, Warning!"* 24; *Sing Out!* November 1965, 105.

47. Seeger quoted in Dunaway, *How Can I Keep from Singing,* 140.

48. Ibid.

49. Sandburg quoted in Cantwell, *When We Were Good,* 178.

50. Seeger quoted in Cantwell, *When We Were Good,* 179.

51. Dick Weissman, *Which Side Are You On? An Inside History of the Folk Music Revival in America* (New York: Continuum, 2005), 66.

52. *Newsweek* quoted in Cohen, *Rainbow Quest,* 79.

53. "Out of the Corner," *Time,* September 25, 1950, 69.

54. Lee Hays, "From The Post-humous 'Memoirs,'" in Hays, *"Sing Out, Warning!"* 105.

55. Winkler interview with Pete and Toshi Seeger, April 18, 2008.

56. Hays, "From 'The Post-humous ' Memoirs,'" 106.

57. Klein, *Woody Guthrie,* 371.

58. Seeger quoted in Dunaway, *How Can I Keep from Singing,* 144.

THREE

1. *Time* quoted in David Dunaway, *How Can I Keep from Singing: Pete Seeger* (New York: Da Capo Press, 1990), 155.

2. This question appeared over and over, in hearing after hearing. Quoted in Allan M. Winkler, *The Cold War: A History in Documents* (New York: Oxford University Press, 2000), 47.

3. Dunaway, *How Can I Keep from Singing,* 151.

4. Kameron and Seeger quoted in Dunaway, *How Can I Keep from Singing,* 149.

5. Seeger quoted in Dunaway, *How Can I Keep from Singing,* 157.

6. Ibid.

7. David Dunaway interview with Pete Seeger, March 6, 1977, Box 1, Folder 9, David Dunaway/Pete Seeger Interviews Collection, Library of Congress.

8. Matusow, quoted in Ronald D. Cohen, *Rainbow Quest: The Folk Music Revival and American Society, 1940–1970* (Amherst: University of Massachusetts Press, 2002), 79.

9. Seeger quoted in Dunaway, *How Can I Keep from Singing,* 156.

10. *Variety* quoted in Dunaway, *How Can I Keep from Singing,* 153.

11. *Downbeat* quoted in Dunaway, *How Can I Keep from Singing,* 153.

12. Seeger quoted in Cohen, *Rainbow Quest,* 77.

13. Gilbert quoted in Cohen, *Rainbow Quest,* 79.

14. Hays quoted in Dunaway, *How Can I Keep from Singing,* 156.

15. Shelton quoted in Cohen, *Rainbow Quest,* 102.

16. Allan M. Winkler interview with Pete Seeger, Beacon, New York, August 3, 2006.

17. Allan M. Winkler interview with Pete and Toshi Seeger, Beacon, New York, April 18, 2008.

18. Seeger quoted in Dunaway, *How Can I Keep from Singing,* 120.

19. McLean quoted in Dunaway, *How Can I Keep from Singing,* 158.

20. Seeger quoted in Dunaway, *How Can I Keep from Singing,* 158.

21. *Providence Journal* quoted in Dunaway, *How Can I Keep from Singing,* 159.

22. Pete Seeger, *Where Have All the Flowers Gone: A Singer's Stories, Songs, Seeds, Robberies* (Bethlehem, Penn.: Sing Out Corporation, 1993), 166; Pete Seeger, © 1961 (Renewed), Sanga Music, Inc. All rights reserved. Used by permission.

23. Ibid., 166–167.

24. David Dunaway interview with Pete Seeger, October 9, 1977, Box 1, Folder 12, David Dunaway/Pete Seeger Interviews Collection. See also Dunaway, *How Can I Keep from Singing,* 164.

25. Lee Hays, *"Sing Out Warning! Sing Out, Love!": The Writings of Lee Hays,* edited by Robert S. Koppelman (Amherst: University of Massachusetts Press, 2003), 116.

26. Hearings before the Committee on Un-American Activities, Investigation of Communist Activities, New York Area—Part VI (Entertainment), House of Representatives, 84th Congress, 1st session, August 15 and 16, 1955 (Washington, D.C.: United States Government Printing Office, 1955), 2350, 2354, 2360.

27. Hays, *"Sing Out Warning!"* 116.

28. Seeger quoted in Dunaway, *How Can I Keep from Singing,* 168.

29. Conversation between Seeger and Ross quoted in Dunaway, *How Can I Keep from Singing,* 171.

30. Hearings before the Committee on Un-American Activities, Investigation of Communist Activities, New York Area—Part VI (Entertainment), House of Representatives, 2448–2450.

31. Pete Seeger, *The Incompleat Folksinger,* edited by Jo Metcalf Schwartz (New York: Simon & Schuster, 1972), 471–472; Lee Hays, Walter Lowenfels © 1957 (Renewed), Sanga Music, Inc. All rights reserved. Used by permission.

32. Hearings before the Committee on Un-American Activities, Investigation of Communist Activities, New York Area—Part VI (Entertainment), House of Representatives, 2451–2452.

33. Bert Alan Spector, "'Wasn't That a Time?': Pete Seeger and the Anti-Communist Crusade, 1940–1968," PhD dissertation, University of Missouri–Columbia, 1977, 164–165.

34. Seeger quoted in Dunaway, *How Can I Keep from Singing,* 190.

35. Winkler interview with Pete Seeger, August 3, 2006.

36. David Dunaway interview with Pete Seeger, October 9, 1977, Box 1, Folder 12, David Dunaway/Pete Seeger Interviews Collection.

37. *Federal Supplement, Volume 180: Cases Argued and Determined in the United States District Courts, United States Court of Claims and the United States Customs Court* (St. Paul, Minn.: West, 1960), 468.

38. *New York Times,* March 15, 1961.

39. *United States of America v. Peter Seeger,* March 27, 28, 29, 1961, Southern District Court Criminal Case File C152–240, pp. 13, 17. See also *New York Times,* March 28, 1961.

40. *New York Times,* March 29, 1961.

41. Reporter quoted in Dunaway, *How Can I Keep from Singing,* 200.

42. *United States of America v. Peter Seeger,* March April 4, 1961, Southern District Court Criminal Case File C152–240, pp. 459–461. See also "Pete Seeger's Statement to the Court, 1961," reprinted from *Sing Out!* Summer 1961, 10–11, at http://www.peteseeger.net/court1961.htm. It also appears in a slightly different version in Seeger, *Incompleat Folksinger,* 470–471.

43. *United States of America, Appellee, v. Peter Seeger, Defendant-Appellant,* No. 293, Docket 27101, United States Court of Appeals, Second Circuit, Argued April 9, 1962, Decided May 18, 1962, *Federal Reporter, Second Series, Volume 303 F.2d: Cases Argued and Determined in the United States Courts of Appeals, United States Court of Claims and United States Court of Customs and Patent Appeals* (St. Paul, Minn.: West, 1962), 481.

44. *New York Post* quoted in Dunaway, *How Can I Keep from Singing,* 210.

45. Jim Brown, *Pete Seeger: The Power of Song* (DVD).

46. "Folk Singing," *Time,* November 23, 1962, 60.

Four

1. Associate producer quoted in David Dunaway, *How Can I Keep from Singing: Pete Seeger* (New York: Da Capo Press, 1990), 215.

2. *San Francisco Chronicle* quoted in Dunaway, *How Can I Keep from Singing,* 215.

3. Lewine quoted in Dunaway, *How Can I Keep from Singing,* 217.

4. Seeger quoted in Dunaway, *How Can I Keep from Singing,* 216.

5. Seeger quoted in Dunaway, *How Can I Keep from Singing,* 217.

6. Lomax quoted in David Hajdu, *Positively 4th Street: The Lives and Times of Joan Baez, Bob Dylan, Mimi Baez Fariña and Richard Fariña* (New York: Farrar, Straus, and Giroux, 2001), 64.

7. Tia Henderson quoted in Hajdu, *Positively 4th Street,* 7.

8. Seeger quoted in Hajdu, *Positively 4th Street,* 8.

9. Ibid.

10. Ibid., 91.

11. Dylan quoted in Dunaway, *How Can I Keep from Singing,* 247.

12. Robert Cantwell, *When We Were Good: The Folk Revival* (Cambridge, Mass.: Harvard University Press, 1996), 296–297.

13. "Leisure: String 'Em Up," *Time,* January 5, 1962, 46.

14. Allan M. Winkler interview with Pete Seeger, Beacon, New York, August 3, 2006.

15. Toshi Seeger quoted in David Dunaway interview with Pete Seeger, October 6, 1976, Box 1, Folder 7, David Dunaway/Pete Seeger Interviews Collection, Library of Congress.

16. Winkler interview with Pete Seeger, August 3, 2006.

17. King quoted in Dunaway, *How Can I Keep from Singing,* 221.

18. Pete Seeger, *Where Have All the Flowers Gone: A Singer's Stories, Songs, Seeds, Robberies* (Bethlehem, Penn.: Sing Out Corporation, 1993), 32–34; Pete Seeger, *The Incompleat Folksinger,* edited by Jo Metcalf Schwartz (New York: Simon & Schuster, 1972), 111–112; Winkler interview with Pete Seeger, August 3, 2006.

19. Seeger quoted in Dunaway, *How Can I Keep from Singing,* 222.

20. Anita Krajnc and Michael Greenspoon, "Singing Together for Social Change: An Interview with Pete Seeger," *Peace Magazine,* July/August 1997, 28. See also John W. Whitehead, "When Will They Ever Learn? An Interview with Pete Seeger," *OldSpeak,* January 4, 2006, at http://www .rutherford.org/Oldspeak/Articles/Art/oldspeak-Seeger.html.

21. Winkler interview with Pete Seeger, August 3, 2006.

22. Ibid.

23. Seeger, *Where Have All the Flowers Gone,* 35.

24. Guy and Candie Carawan, "'Freedom in the Air': An Overview of the Songs of the Civil Rights Movement," *Black Music Research Bulletin,* vol. 12, no. 1 (Spring 1990): 1.

25. Ibid., 2.

26. Ibid.

27. Introduction to "Oh, Mary, Don't You Weep," *The Best of Pete Seeger* (CD), Vanguard Records, 1994.

28. Winkler interview with Pete Seeger, August 3, 2006.

29. "Oh, Mary, Don't You Weep," *The Best of Pete Seeger* (CD).

30. Toshi Seeger quoted in Dunaway, *How Can I Keep from Singing,* 225.

31. Taylor Branch, *Parting the Waters: America in the King Years, 1954–1963* (New York: Simon & Schuster, 1988), 718.

32. Conversation quoted in Dunaway, *How Can I Keep from Singing,* 222.

33. Seeger quoted in Dunaway, *How Can I Keep from Singing,* 227.

34. Ibid., 223–224, 229.

35. *New Delhi Statesman* quoted in Dunaway, *How Can I Keep from Singing,* 230.

36. Toshi Seeger quoted in Dunaway, *How Can I Keep from Singing,* 231.

37. Seeger quoted in Dunaway, *How Can I Keep from Singing,* 231.

38. Exchange quoted in Dunaway, *How Can I Keep from Singing,* 234, refined by Seeger in conversation with Allan M. Winkler, May 29, 2008.

39. Schoolteacher quoted in Dunaway, *How Can I Keep from Singing,* 234.

40. Pete Seeger, "Johnny Appleseed, Jr.," *Sing Out!* November 1964, 91; Dunaway, *How Can I Keep from Singing,* 235; Fred Hellerman, Fran Minkoff © 1964 (Renewed), Appleseed, Inc. All rights reserved. Used by permission.

41. Seeger quoted in Dunaway, *How Can I Keep from Singing,* 235.

42. King quoted in Harvard Sitkoff, *The Struggle for Black Equality, 1954–1992,* revised edition (New York: Hill and Wang, 1993), 174.

43. *Sing Out!* July 1965, 11.

44. David Kupfer, "A Conversation with Pete Seeger," unpublished transcript, 2004, in Seeger's possession.

FIVE

1. David Dunaway, *How Can I Keep from Singing: Pete Seeger* (New York: Da Capo Press, 1990), 246.

2. David Kupfer, "Long Time Passing: An Interview with Pete Seeger," *Spring 2001 Whole Earth Catalog,* 21; Allan M. Winkler conversation with Pete Seeger, May 29, 2008.

3. Pete Seeger, *The Incompleat Folksinger,* edited by Jo Metcalf Schwartz (New York: Simon & Schuster, 1972), 553; Benjamin Filene, *Romancing the*

Folk: Public Memory and American Roots Music (Chapel Hill: University of North Carolina Press, 2000), 203.

4. Pete Seeger, *Where Have All the Flowers Gone: A Singer's Stories, Songs, Seeds, Robberies* (Bethlehem, Penn.: Sing Out Corporation, 1993), 147.

5. Allan M. Winkler interview with Pete Seeger, Beacon, New York, August 3, 2006.

6. Baez, quoted in David Hajdu, *Positively 4th Street: The Lives and Times of Joan Baez, Bob Dylan, Mimi Baez Fariña and Richard Fariña* (New York: Farrar, Straus, and Giroux, 2001), 199.

7. Seeger, *Where Have All the Flowers Gone,* 148; Pete Seeger, © 1965 (Renewed), Sanga Music, Inc. All rights reserved. Used by permission.

8. Ibid., 147.

9. Dunaway, *How Can I Keep from Singing,* 250.

10. *New York Times,* October 25, 1965.

11. Seeger, *Where Have All the Flowers Gone,* 148.

12. Ibid.

13. Ibid.

14. Lyndon B. Johnson, quoted in Charles E. Neu, *America's Lost War: Vietnam: 1945–1975* (Wheeling, Ill.: Harlan Davidson, 2005), 81.

15. David Farber, *The Age of Great Dreams: America in the 1960s* (New York: Hill and Wang, 1994), 156–157.

16. Seeger quoted in Dunaway, *How Can I Keep from Singing,* 256.

17. Poem quoted in Dunaway, *How Can I Keep from Singing,* 262

18. Seeger, *Where Have All the Flowers Gone,* 149; Pete Seeger, © 1966 (Renewed), Stormking Music, Inc. All rights reserved. Used by permission.

19. Ibid.

20. Ibid.

21. Winkler conversation with Seeger, May 29, 2008.

22. Seeger, *Where Have All the Flowers Gone,* 150.

23. Seeger quoted in Dunaway, *How Can I Keep from Singing,* 252.

24. George C. Herring, *America's Longest War: The United States and Vietnam, 1950–1975* (New York: Wiley, 1979), 134.

25. Johnson, quoted in Farber, *The Age of Great Dreams*, 134.

26. Seeger, *Where Have All the Flowers Gone*, 149, 151.

27. Staffer quoted in ibid., 149–150.

28. Ibid., 149.

29. *Los Angeles Times* quoted in Dunaway, *How Can I Keep from Singing*, 262.

30. *New York Times*, August 25, 1967; *New York Times*, September 4, 1967.

31. Seeger quoted in Dunaway, *How Can I Keep from Singing*, 263.

32. Seeger, *Where Have All the Flowers Gone*, 149.

33. Seeger quoted in Dunaway, *How Can I Keep from Singing*, 263.

34. "Big and Muddy," *Newsweek*, September 25, 1967, 118.

35. *Variety* and *New York Times* quoted in Dunaway, *How Can I Keep from Singing*, 264; "Television This Week," *New York Times*, September 10, 1967.

36. Seeger quoted in Dunaway, *How Can I Keep from Singing*, 264.

37. Seeger, *Where Have All the Flowers Gone*, 149.

38. "Big and Muddy," 118.

39. Farber, *Age of Great Dreams*, 212–215.

40. Johnson quoted in Mark Hamilton Lytle, *America's Uncivil Wars: The Sixties Era from Elvis to the Fall of Richard Nixon* (New York: Oxford University Press, 2006), 250.

41. Seeger quoted in Dunaway, *How Can I Keep from Singing*, 274–275.

42. Reagon quoted in Dunaway, *How Can I Keep from Singing*, 276.

43. David Dunaway interview with Pete Seeger, December 15, 1977, Box 1, Folder 14, David Dunaway/Pete Seeger Interviews Collection, Library of Congress.

44. © 1969 (Renewed 1997) Sony/ATV Tunes LLC. All rights administered by Sony/ATV Music Publishing, 8 Music Square West, Nashville, TN 37203

45. Seeger, *Where Have All the Flowers Gone,* 156–157.

46. Winkler interview with Pete Seeger, August 3, 2006.

47. Seeger, *Where Have All the Flowers Gone,* 160.

Six

1. Allan M. Winkler interview with Pete Seeger, Beacon, New York, August 3, 2006.

2. Matthew Purdy, "Waist Deep in a Cleaner Hudson, an Old Folkie Pushes On," *New York Times,* June 22, 2001.

3. Rachel Carson, *Silent Spring* (New York: Fawcett World Library, 1962), 16.

4. Winkler interview with Pete Seeger, August 3, 2006.

5. Pete Seeger, quoted in the documentary *'Til the River Runs Clear: Pete Seeger and the* Clearwater, Kunhardt Productions (PBS Home Video, 2007).

6. Winkler interview with Pete Seeger, August 3, 2006.

7. Pete Seeger, *Where Have All the Flowers Gone: A Singer's Stories, Songs, Seeds, Robberies* (Bethlehem, Penn.: Sing Out Corporation, 1993), 201.

8. Linda C. Forbes, "Possibility and Hope: Getting from Here to There," *Monthly Review,* January 2005, at http://www.monthlyreview.org/0105seeger.htm.

9. *'Til the River Runs Clear: Pete Seeger and the* Clearwater.

10. Seeger, *Where Have All the Flowers Gone,* 201.

11. *'Til the River Runs Clear: Pete Seeger and the* Clearwater.

12. Seeger, *Where Have All the Flowers Gone,* 202; Pete Seeger, © 1964 (Renewed), Sanga Music, Inc. All rights reserved. Used by permission.

13. Ibid., 202–203.

14. David Dunaway interview with Pete Seeger, August 8, 1978, Box 2, Folder 15, David Dunaway/Pete Seeger Interviews Collection, Library of Congress.

15. Seeger, *Where Have All the Flowers Gone,* 205.

16. Seeger quoted in David Dunaway, *How Can I Keep from Singing: Pete Seeger* (New York: Da Capo Press, 1990), 250.

17. Seeger, *Where Have All the Flowers Gone,* 206.

18. Seeger quoted in Dunaway, *How Can I Keep from Singing,* 282.

19. Ibid.

20. *'Til the River Runs Clear: Pete Seeger and the* Clearwater.

21. Seeger, *Where Have All the Flowers Gone,* 205.

22. Quoted in Dunaway, *How Can I Keep from Singing,* 284.

23. Jim Brown, *Pete Seeger: The Power of Song* (New York: Concert Productions International, 2007).

24. Quoted in Dunaway, *How Can I Keep from Singing,* 284.

25. Forbes, "Possibility and Hope."

26. *'Til the River Runs Clear: Pete Seeger and the* Clearwater.

27. David Dunaway interview with Pete Seeger, August 8, 1978, Box 2, Folder 15, David Dunaway/Pete Seeger Interviews Collection.

28. Allan M. Winkler interview with Pete Seeger, Beacon, New York, December 7, 2007.

29. *'Til the River Runs Clear: Pete Seeger and the* Clearwater.

30. David Dunaway interview with Pete Seeger, August 8, 1978, Box 2, Folder 15, David Dunaway/Pete Seeger Interviews Collection.

31. Quoted in Forbes, "Possibility and Hope."

32. Pete Seeger, "To Save the Dying Hudson: Pete Seeger's Voyage," *Look,* August 26, 1969, 63–65.

33. Ibid., 63.

34. Seeger quoted in Dunaway, *How Can I Keep from Singing,* 288.

35. Ibid., 289.

36. Seeger, "To Save the Dying Hudson," 65.

37. David Dunaway interview with Pete Seeger, August 8, 1978, Box 2, Folder 15, David Dunaway/Pete Seeger Interviews Collection.

38. Seeger, *Where Have All the Flowers Gone,* 208–209.

39. Ibid., 223. Pete Seeger, © 1974, Sanga Music, Inc. All rights reserved. Used by permission.

40. Ibid., 140–141.

41. Winkler interview with Pete Seeger, December 7, 2007.

42. Seeger quoted in Forbes, "Possibility and Hope."

43. *'Til the River Runs Clear: Pete Seeger and the* Clearwater. See also David Dunaway interview with Pete Seeger, August 8, 1978, Box 2, Folder 15, David Dunaway/Pete Seeger Interviews Collection.

44. Quoted in Dunaway, *How Can I Keep from Singing,* 292.

45. Scott Harris, "Pete Seeger: Folk Music's Granddad Plays It Green," *E Magazine: The Environmental Magazine,* November/December 1994.

46. *New York Times,* November 6, 1986, October 9, 1994.

47. William J. Clinton, *Public Papers of the Presidents of the United States: 1994:* Book 2 (Washington, D.C.: U.S. Government Printing Office, 1995), 1762, 1764.

48. Kennedy Center Honors, The John F. Kennedy Center for the Performing Arts, "Remarks by the President at Kennedy Center Honors Reception," press release, December 4, 1994, Washington, D.C. See also the documentary by Jim Brown, *Pete Seeger: The Power of Song.*

49. "Pete Seeger: '94 K.C. Honors," DVD provided by Kennedy Center Honors, The John F. Kennedy Center for the Performing Arts, Washington, D.C.

50. Pete Seeger, appreciation page, at http://www.peteseeger.net/.

51. Seeger quoted in David King Dunaway, *How Can I Keep from Singing? The Ballad of Pete Seeger* (New York: Villard Books, 2008), 414.

52. Seeger, *Where Have All the Flowers Gone,* 82–83; Pete Seeger, © 1970, Sanga Music, Inc. All rights reserved. Used by permission.

AFTERWORD

1. Jim Brown, *Pete Seeger: The Power of Song* (DVD).

2. Rodriguez quoted in Tony Vellela, "Music Meets Environment at Clearwater Revival Festival," *Christian Science Monitor,* June 23, 1995.

3. Pete Seeger, *Where Have All the Flowers Gone: A Singer's Stories, Songs, Seeds, Robberies* (Bethlehem, Penn.: Sing Out Corporation, 1993), 184.

4. "Deep Blue Sea" on the CD *The Best of Pete Seeger*, Vanguard Records, 1994.

5. *'Til the River Runs Clear: Pete Seeger and the* Clearwater, Kunhardt Productions (PBS Home Video, 2007).

6. David Dunaway, *How Can I Keep from Singing: Pete Seeger* (New York: Da Capo Press, 1990), preface.

7. Seeger's annotated copy of Dunaway, *How Can I Keep from Singing.*

8. Pete Seeger, *The Incompleat Folksinger,* edited by Jo Metcalf Schwartz (New York: Simon & Schuster, 1972), 563.

9. Seeger quoted in Dunaway, *How Can I Keep from Singing,* 227.

10. Seeger, *Incompleat Folksinger,* 260.

11. *Pete Seeger's Storysong Abiyoyo,* illustrated by Michael Hays (New York: Simon & Schuster Books for Young Readers, 2001).

12. Seeger, *Where Have All the Flowers Gone,* 134.

13. Seeger, *Incompleat Folksinger,* 330.

14. Scott Simon, "Interview: Folk Singer Pete Seeger Talks about His Career Writing and Singing Folk Music," *Weekend Edition,* National Public Radio, July 2, 2005.

15. Seeger, *Incompleat Folksinger,* 331–332.

16. Arlo Guthrie, "Garden Song," on *Precious Friend*, Disc 2, Warner Bros. Records, Inc, 1982.

17. Cooney quoted in Dunaway, *How Can I Keep from Singing,* 207.

18. Peggy Seeger quoted in Dunaway, *How Can I Keep from Singing,* 207.

19. *Sing Out!* Summer 1960, 41.

20. "Making Music, Making Waves: Pete Seeger Interviewed by Joe Fahey, July 8, 1995," *Fellowship,* May/June 1996, 8.

21. Brown, *Pete Seeger: The Power of Song.*

22. Ibid.

23. Studs Terkel, "Pete Seeger Is 86," *The Nation,* May 16, 2005.

24. Pete Seeger, "Whatever Happened to Singing in the Unions?" *Sing Out!* May 1965, 31.

25. Douglass quoted in Geoffrey Green, "Time Capsule: Interview with Pete Seeger (1968)," *Interdisciplinary Humanities,* April 2003, 72.

26. Seeger quoted in *New York Times,* January 22, 1995.

27. Toshi Seeger quoted in Brown, *Pete Seeger: The Power of Song.*

28. Seeger, *Where Have All the Flowers Gone,* 261.

29. Benjamin Filene, *Romancing the Folk: Public Memory and American Roots Music* (Chapel Hill: University of North Carolina Press, 2000), 201–203.

30. Seeger, *Where Have All the Flowers Gone,* 54.

31. Toshi Seeger quoted in Brown, *Pete Seeger: The Power of Song.*

32. Allan M. Winkler interview with Pete and Toshi Seeger, Beacon, New York, April 18, 2008.

33. David Kupfer, "A Conversation with Pete Seeger," unpublished transcript, 2004, in Seeger's possession.

34. "Using Music to Change the World: Pete Seeger Speaks with Tom Chapin," *Why,* Summer 1998, 12.

35. John Seeger quoted in Brown, *Pete Seeger: The Power of Song.*

36. Seeger quoted in Dunaway, *How Can I Keep from Singing,* 306.

37. Springsteen quoted in Brown, *Pete Seeger: The Power of Song.*

38. "Using Music to Change the World," 10.

39. Seeger, *Where Have All the Flowers Gone,* 172; Allan M. Winkler interview with Pete Seeger, Beacon, New York, December 7, 2007.

Selected Bibliography

BOOKS BY PETE SEEGER

Seeger, Pete. *The Incompleat Folksinger*. Ed. Jo Metcalf Schwartz. New York: Simon & Schuster, 1972.

———. *Where Have All the Flowers Gone: A Singer's Stories, Songs, Seeds, Robberies*. Ed. Peter Blood. Bethlehem, Penn.: Sing Out Corporation, 1993.

———. *Where Have All the Flowers Gone: A Singalong Memoir*. Ed. Michael Miller and Sarah A. Elisabeth. Bethlehem, Penn.: Sing Out! Publications, 2009.

BOOKS ABOUT PETE SEEGER

Dunaway, David. *How Can I Keep from Singing: Pete Seeger*. New York: Da Capo Press, 1990.

———. *How Can I Keep from Singing? The Ballad of Pete Seeger*. New York: Villard Books, 2008.

BOOKS ABOUT FOLK MUSIC

Cantwell, Robert. *When We Were Good: The Folk Revival*. Cambridge, Mass.: Harvard University Press, 1996.

Cohen, Ronald D. *Rainbow Quest: The Folk Music Revival and American Society, 1940–1970*. Amherst: University of Massachusetts Press, 2002.

Denisoff, R. Serge. *Great Day Coming: Folk Music and the American Left*. Urbana: University of Illinois Press, 1971.

Filene, Benjamin. *Romancing the Folk: Public Memory and American Roots Music*. Chapel Hill: University of North Carolina Press, 2000.

Hajdu, David. *Positively 4th Street: The Lives and Times of Joan Baez, Bob Dylan, Mimi Baez Fariña and Richard Fariña*. New York: Farrar, Straus, and Giroux, 2001.

Hard Hitting Songs for Hard-Hit People. Compiled by Alan Lomax. Notes on the songs by Woody Guthrie, music transcribed and edited by Pete Seeger. New York: Oak Publications, 1967.

Hays, Lee. *"Sing Out, Warning! Sing Out, Love!" The Writings of Lee Hays*. Ed. Robert S. Koppelman. Amherst: University of Massachusetts Press, 2003.

Jackson, Mark Allan. *Prophet Singer: The Voice and Vision of Woody Guthrie*. Jackson: University Press of Mississippi, 2007.

Klein, Joe. *Woody Guthrie: A Life*. New York: Ballantine Books, 1986.

Lankford, Ronald D., Jr. *Folk Music USA: The Changing Voice of Protest*. New York: Schirmer Trade Books, 2005.

Lynch, Timothy P. *Strike Songs of the Depression*. Jackson: University Press of Mississippi, 2001.

Robinson, Tiny, and John Reynolds, eds. *Lead Belly: A Life in Pictures*. Göttingen, Germany: Steidl, 2008.

Weissman, Dick. *Which Side Are You On? An Inside History of the Folk Music Revival in America*. New York: Continuum International, 2005.

Index

Page numbers in *italics* indicate photographs and illustrations.